Harry Potter™

CHARACTERS OF THE MAGICAL WORLD

WRITTEN BY
JON RICHARDS

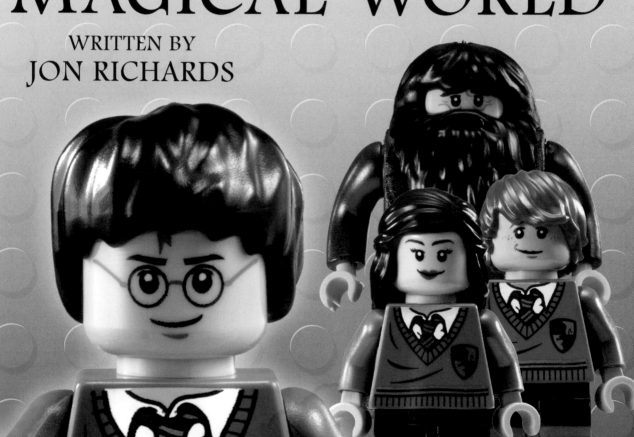

Contents

— MEET THE MINIFIGURES —

INTRODUCTION

Minifigures are at the heart of all of the LEGO® Harry Potter™ sets – from Harry, Ron and Hermione, to Hogwarts professors and the villainous Voldemort. As the characters developed throughout the films, the minifigures also evolved – with versions depicting their changing faces and outfits, and featuring LEGO innovations such as flesh tones and double-sided heads. To create the sets starring Harry and his minifigure friends, the LEGO Group has also designed a host of magical creatures, from dragons to phoenixes, and accompanying accessories made from unique, highly collectible LEGO elements.

How to use this book:

This book is divided into seven chapters, each following one of Harry's seven years at Hogwarts – from *Harry Potter and the Philosopher's Stone* through to *Harry Potter and the Deathly Hallows*. All minifigures were released with sets recreating events from the films (with the exception of two exclusives created for Dorling Kindersley books).

The minifigures in this book are ordered according to the set in which they first appeared or mostly feature. Hagrid, for instance, appears in many LEGO Harry Potter sets, but his first appearance is with the first Hagrid's hut set, based on *Harry Potter and the Philosopher's Stone*, and so he can be found in the first chapter.

The book also distinguishes between "versions" of minifigures and "variants". Versions are separate minifigures in their own right, while variants are the same version of a minifigure but with modifications. For example, there are many variants of Harry wearing his Gryffindor uniform but there are also versions of his minifigure wearing swimming trunks, his Quidditch outfit and plain blue clothes (see right).

This book features all variants and versions released by the LEGO Group. All variants are pictured in variant boxes on the minifigure's page. The main image is usually the most recent variation of a minifigure.

Data File boxes on every page detail the number of LEGO pieces from which a minifigure is made, any accessories the minifigure carries and the sets a minifigure was released in, along with the year that the set was released.

Harry's snowy owl, Hedwig, features feather patterns and printing unique to LEGO Harry Potter.

A wand is an essential LEGO Harry Potter accessory, made from a standard LEGO® *Star Wars*™ lightsaber piece.

Harry's unique hair piece appears on every one of his minifigure variants.

This luggage trunk can carry all manner of accessory tiles – from those representing a newspaper and bedding, to a magical flute.

5

Unique Elements

Most **LEGO®** minifigures are made up of four basic pieces: legs, torso, head and hair. Some elements are essential, while others vary from minifigure to minifigure. Many of these features have been uniquely created for the LEGO® Harry Potter™ theme, while others received exclusive printing or original colours.

Hat

WIZARD'S HAT

This hat is common across many LEGO sets, but Professor McGonagall is the only Harry Potter minifigure to wear it in dark green.

Heads

HOUSE-ELF

Dobby's unique head was moulded especially in flexible rubber, with printed green eyes in this 2010 variant.

GOBLIN

The first LEGO goblins appeared in sets 4714 and 10217. Their head pieces appear only in LEGO Harry Potter.

SHARK

The LEGO Group created this sand blue shark's head for Viktor Krum to wear over his minifigure head in set 4762.

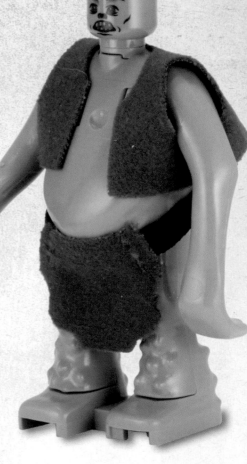

TROLL

With the exception of its head and club, the troll from set 4712 uses pieces that are found nowhere else in the LEGO Harry Potter theme, or even in the LEGO universe.

Cloaks

DEMENTOR'S ROBE
This tattered black cloak has made two ghoulish appearances – in two versions of Hogwarts (sets 4842 and 4867).

GREY ROBE
This grey cloth robe was specially designed to cloak Death Eater and Voldemort minifigures.

WIZARD'S ROBE
This starry robe is unique to LEGO Harry Potter, and has been worn by ten minifigures, including Draco and Harry.

QUIDDITCH ROBE
Only flying teacher Madam Hooch wears this exclusive black and white striped cloak, for set 4726.

Hair

HARRY
This iconic black hair piece was designed especially for Harry Potter and features on all of his minifigures.

BELLATRIX
Bellatrix Lestrange's highly elaborate and detailed hair piece appears only in one LEGO set (4840).

HAGRID
Hagrid's oversized minifigure requires an equally oversized single hair and beard piece.

GINNY
Uniquely coloured hair pieces were produced for the Weasley family, such as Ginny's 2010 variants.

Lower body

SKIRT
This skirt was designed for Professor McGonagall. Sloped pieces are found on six other Harry Potter minifigures.

PEG-LEG
LEGO peg-legs are usually brown. Mad-Eye Moody was the first minifigure to receive this false leg in silver.

DEMENTOR
This clever piece of LEGO design gives the impression that Dementor minifigures can actually fly.

MERPERSON TAIL
LEGO merpeople have uniquely printed tails. This merperson minifigure appears in set 4762.

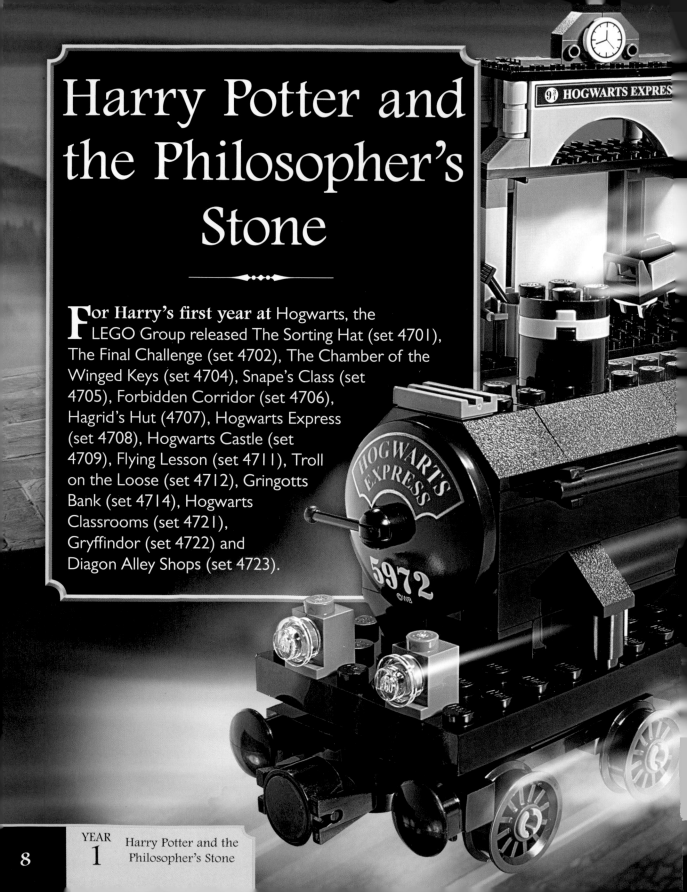

Harry Potter and the Philosopher's Stone

For Harry's first year at Hogwarts, the LEGO Group released The Sorting Hat (set 4701), The Final Challenge (set 4702), The Chamber of the Winged Keys (set 4704), Snape's Class (set 4705), Forbidden Corridor (set 4706), Hagrid's Hut (4707), Hogwarts Express (set 4708), Hogwarts Castle (set 4709), Flying Lesson (set 4711), Troll on the Loose (set 4712), Gringotts Bank (set 4714), Hogwarts Classrooms (set 4721), Gryffindor (set 4722) and Diagon Alley Shops (set 4723).

Harry Potter and the
Philosopher's Stone

Harry Potter
— THE BOY WHO LIVED —

Harry Potter is ready for his first year at Hogwarts School of Witchcraft and Wizardry. Dressed in his casual clothes, he's about to board the Hogwarts Express (set 4708) for the long trip to the school. In total, there are 24 different minifigures of Harry.

Every minifigure of Harry bears his iconic lightning-shaped scar.

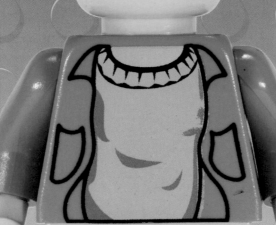

Wand
Harry's 2004 minifigure (below) comes with its own black wand. Attached to the end of this is a special transparent cone piece. This represents a *Lumos* spell, which Harry can use to light his way in the dark.

DATA FILE

SETS: 4708 Hogwarts Express (2001), 4714 Gringotts Bank (2002)
PIECES: 4
ACCESSORIES: Brown wand, black suitcase, luggage cart

The LEGO Group used traditional yellow hands and faces for all Harry Potter minifigures until 2004.

VARIANTS

SETS: 4755 Knight Bus (2004)
PIECES: 4
ACCESSORIES: Black wand with *Lumos* spell, bedroll tile, chest

YEAR 1   Harry Potter and the Philosopher's Stone

Rubeus Hagrid
HALF-GIANT GAMEKEEPER

Hagrid's head has wrinkles and a shaggy beard piece.

Hagrid's super-sized legs are unposeable.

Hogwarts' gamekeeper Hagrid is a half-giant, so the LEGO Group has created a not-so-mini minifigure to suit his large form. There are three variants in total, appearing in eight different sets. Each stands a whole head taller than his minifigure friends.

The 2010 Hagrid has movable hands with moulded fingers and thumbs instead of brown gloves (below).

VARIANTS

SETS: 4707 Hagrid's Hut (2001), 4709 Hogwarts Castle (2001), 4714 Gringotts Bank (2002)
PIECES: 3
ACCESSORIES: Axe, pickaxe, torch, key

SETS: 4754 Hagrid's Hut (2004), 5378 Hogwarts Castle (2007)
PIECES: 3
ACCESSORIES: Barrel of tools, key, crossbow

DATA FILE

SETS: 4738 Hagrid's Hut (2010), 10217 Diagon Alley (2011), 4865 The Forbidden Forest (2011)
PIECES: 3
ACCESSORIES: Umbrella wand, crossbow

Gringotts goblins
⟩⟩•⟩ GOBLIN BANK TELLERS ⟩•⟨⟨

The vaults at Gringotts bank are the safest place for a wizard to store any important treasures. LEGO® designers have created two versions of the bank (sets 4714 and 10217) and staffed them with these smartly dressed goblin minifigures to work behind the bank's counters.

DATA FILE

SETS: 4714 Gringotts Bank (2002)
PIECES: 3
ACCESSORIES: Dark grey money tile

Early goblins have cream-coloured heads.

This goblin with a red jacket and black trousers represents Griphook.

Money tile
As well as shiny gold coins (p.136), Gringotts Bank (set 4714) contains tile pieces printed with mysterious parcels and bags of money, all kept secure in the Gringotts vaults.

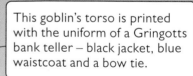

This goblin's torso is printed with the uniform of a Gringotts bank teller – black jacket, blue waistcoat and a bow tie.

The short goblin legs are unposeable, like Dobby's (p.39) and Professor Flitwick's (p.110).

DATA FILE

SETS: 4714 Gringotts Bank (2002)
PIECES: 3
ACCESSORIES: Gold coins

YEAR 1   Harry Potter and the Philosopher's Stone

The 2011 minifigure was released with a flesh-coloured head.

DATA FILE

◆◆◆

SETS: 10217 Diagon Alley (2011)
PIECES: 3
ACCESSORIES: None

New bank

As part of set 10217, the updated version of Gringotts is a more detailed creation than the earlier model. It features ornate columns and a candelabra.

This minifigure variant with reddish-brown trousers represents Griphook.

Did you know?
In Gringotts Bank (set 4714), Griphook drives the underground train that carries Harry and Hagrid down to the bank's vaults.

Unlike most other LEGO minifigures, the Gringotts goblins do not have printed eyes.

DATA FILE

◆◆◆

SETS: 10217 Diagon Alley (2011)
PIECES: 3
ACCESSORIES: None

The 2011 variants of the goblins now wear matching grey waistcoats.

The 2011 variants of the Gringotts goblin use the same torso piece as Professor Flitwick (p.110).

Uniforms

All of the students at Hogwarts are required to wear a uniform during school hours. The same rules apply within the LEGO® Harry Potter™ sets, as minifigures were released wearing uniforms for Quidditch and even the Triwizard Tournament. During class time, however, they are usually found wearing the colours of one of the school's four houses: Gryffindor, Slytherin, Hufflepuff and Ravenclaw. LEGO designers have replicated the smallest details onto the minifigures – printing striped ties, Hogwarts house crests and even tiny creases in the grey material!

General uniform

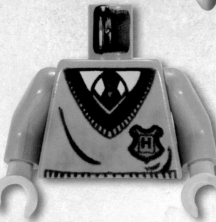

When they first arrive, minifigures wear a general Hogwarts uniform, with a golden "H" crest. This is before they have been sorted into a school house by the Sorting Hat (p.19).

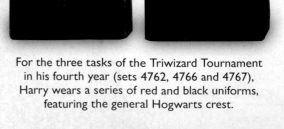

For the three tasks of the Triwizard Tournament in his fourth year (sets 4762, 4766 and 4767), Harry wears a series of red and black uniforms, featuring the general Hogwarts crest.

Gryffindor

For their first and second years, Harry and his friends wear this uniform. It features the Gryffindor crest with the lion of Godric Gryffindor and a thick-striped tie.

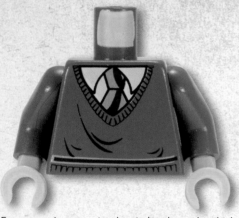

For years three to six, the tie has kept the thick scarlet and gold stripes, but the jumper is plain and does not feature the house crest.

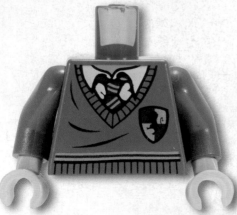

For the last LEGO Harry Potter sets, the Gryffindor uniform has reintroduced the crest, and the tie now features thin gold stripes.

Slytherin

As with Gryffindor, Slytherin's uniform has a thick-striped tie featuring the house colours of silver and green and the coiled snake crest of Salazar Slytherin.

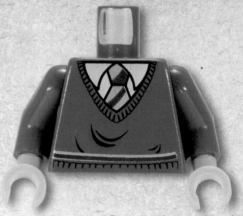

For years three to six, Draco Malfoy and the other members of Slytherin house wear this uniform, with thick tie stripes and no house crest.

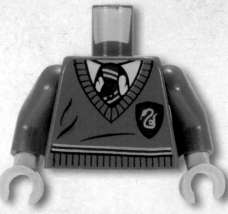

Year seven sees the Slytherin crest return to Draco's uniform, and the tie now features thin silver stripes.

Hermione Granger
⤞ DIAGON ALLEY SHOPPER ⤝

Preparing for Hogwarts, Hermione Granger needs to stock up on wizarding school supplies. In the wizarding world these can all be found in Diagon Alley Shops (set 4723). In this set, she is accompanied by her pet cat, Crookshanks.

DATA FILE

SETS: 4723 Diagon Alley Shops (2001)
PIECES: 4
ACCESSORIES: White tile with spider and bag pattern, coloured wands

Hermione's unique torso is printed with a knitted jumper.

There are nine variants of Hermione's minifigure, but only two are dressed in casual clothing.

Wizard supplies

The Diagon Alley Shops (set 4723) contain everything a student of witchcraft and wizardry could need. This includes transparent coloured wands, cloaks, brooms, wizard hats and pets.

Dressed in her casual blue outfit, this minifigure of Hermione is unique to the Diagon Alley Shops (set 4723).

YEAR 1   Harry Potter and the Philosopher's Stone

Ron Weasley
❖ HARRY'S BEST FRIEND ❖

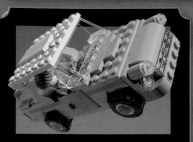

Flying car
This minifigure of Ron also appears in Escape from Privet Drive (set 4728), recreating events from *Harry Potter and the Chamber of Secrets*. Here, he rescues Harry in a rather unique way – using the Weasleys' flying car!

When Harry is in trouble, he knows he can rely on his friend Ron Weasley. They travel to Hogwarts onboard the Hogwarts Express (set 4708), casually dressed and with pre-school nerves.

The first six minifigures of Ron feature the same grinning face. This was replaced with a new expression in 2005 (p.90).

Ron's minifigure is dressed in casual clothes with an open-necked shirt and blue jumper.

When Ron arrives in Gryffindor (set 4722), he wears the same casual outfit, but with an added cloak (below).

DATA FILE
SETS: 4708 Hogwarts Express (2001), 4728 Escape from Privet Drive (2002)
PIECES: 4
ACCESSORIES: Brown suitcase, light grey wand

VARIANTS

SETS: 4722 Gryffindor (2001)
PIECES: 5
ACCESSORIES: Transparent light blue wand, red suitcase, cloak

The Sorting Hat (set 4701) depicts the ceremony during which new pupils are sorted into one of the four houses of Hogwarts. The set shows Harry wearing his first Hogwarts school uniform and the Sorting Hat. The hat will sort Harry into Gryffindor.

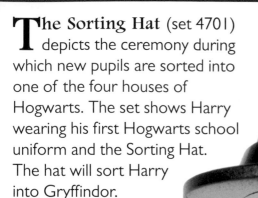

Spin table
To choose which house he will be in, Harry's minifigure sits on top of a large, spinning disc. This is decorated with the crests of all four Hogwarts houses: Gryffindor, Ravenclaw, Hufflepuff and Slytherin.

Harry's hair piece must be removed in order to fit the Sorting Hat on his head.

Harry wears a general Hogwarts uniform as he is not yet a member of Gryffindor.

Harry's minifigure wears a cloak that is decorated with grey stars (see also p.22).

DATA FILE
◆━◆◆◆━◆

SETS: 4701 Sorting Hat (2001)
PIECES: 5
ACCESSORIES: Black cloak, brown wand, white tile with scroll pattern

Sorting Hat
A MAGICAL HAT

DATA FILE

SETS: 4842 Hogwarts
Castle (2010)
PIECES: 1
ACCESSORIES: None

The **Sorting Hat** makes its first magical appearance in *Harry Potter and the Philosopher's Stone*. In 2010, the old, crumpled hat received a new design for Hogwarts Castle (set 4842). LEGO designers changed the colour and added facial details, including a mouth, to match the face-like appearance of the Hat in the films.

The hat features a buckle and band detail around the base.

The reddish-brown hat is printed with fabric creases to make up its face.

The reddish-brown version of the hat is unique to the 2010 Hogwarts Castle (set 4842).

The 2010 Sorting Hat sits on the second floor of Dumbledore's office in Hogwarts.

VARIANTS

SETS: 4701 Sorting Hat (2001), 4729 Dumbledore's Office (2002), 4730 Chamber of Secrets (2002)
PIECES: 1
ACCESSORIES: None

Did you know?
The first variant of the Sorting Hat from set 4730 holds the sword of Gryffindor (p.61).

Hermione Granger

COURAGEOUS GRYFFINDOR

Creeping into the sinister chambers of the Forbidden Corridor (set 4706), Hermione, Ron and Harry must try to get past Fluffy, the three-headed dog, and the Devil's Snare plant. Fortunately, this minifigure comes with a blue flame torch to light their way through the Corridor.

Hermione has the same torso as the minifigures of Ron and Harry from the same year (p.22).

Just like Harry's cloak (p.18), Hermione's is decorated with stars.

VARIANTS

SETS: 4708 Hogwarts Express (2001)
PIECES: 5
ACCESSORIES: Tan wand, green book, cloak

Now that she has gone through the Sorting Ceremony, Hermione's uniform features the Gryffindor crest. Her variant (above) still features the general Hogwarts crest.

DATA FILE

SETS: 4706 Forbidden Corridor (2001), 4709 Hogwarts Castle (2001)
PIECES: 5
ACCESSORIES: Cloak, blue flame torch, tan wand, spell tile

YEAR 1   Harry Potter and the Philosopher's Stone

Professor Dumbledore
◄•◄ HOGWARTS HEADMASTER ►•►

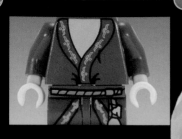

Professor Dumbledore is the Headmaster of Hogwarts School of Witchcraft and Wizardry. He features in four minifigures, the first two of which are dressed in bright purple robes.

Under the beard
Beneath Dumbledore's flowing beard, LEGO designers have kept the ornate details of his robes, complete with gold embroidery.

DATA FILE
◄•◄—•—►•►
SETS: 4757 Hogwarts Castle (2004)
PIECES: 6
ACCESSORIES: Cloak

The 2004 figure has light bluish-grey hair and beard, rather than the light grey hair used on the 2001 variant.

This variant comes with a light purple cloak, while the variant's is a darker purple (below).

VARIANTS
◄•◄—•—►•►

SETS: 4707 Hagrid's Hut (2001), 4709 Hogwarts Castle (2001), 4729 Dumbledore's Office (2002)
PIECES: 6
ACCESSORIES: Cloak, yellow goblet, red book, letter tile

Dumbledore's unique hips and legs are printed with brightly coloured belts and wizarding gadgets.

Harry Potter
◄━━► WIZARD PUPIL ◄━━►

During his first two years at Hogwarts School of Witchcraft and Wizardry, this minifigure of Harry has to face many tests, including battling his fellow pupils in the Duelling Club (set 4733) and learning to ride a broom in Flying Lesson (set 4711).

Harry's cloak is decorated with stars.

DATA FILE
◄━━►

SETS: 4704 The Chamber of the Winged Keys (2001), 4702 The Final Challenge (2001), 4730 Chamber of Secrets (2002), 4729 Dumbledore's Office (2002), 4711 Flying Lesson (2002), 4733 The Duelling Club (2002), 4712 Troll on the Loose (2002)
PIECES: 5
ACCESSORIES: Brown wand, brown broom, winged key, cloak

After the Sorting Ceremony (p.18), Harry wears his Gryffindor uniform.

Did you know?
This minifigure appears in seven LEGO Harry Potter sets – more than any other minifigure.

Grey hips and legs feature on all uniformed Harry Potter minifigures from 2001.

Harry Potter
VIOLET CLOAK

In the Hogwarts Classrooms (set 4721), Harry sets about mixing potions and practising his magic skills in the Potions classroom. To make him stand out from other Harry minifigures, LEGO designers have given this variant a bright violet-coloured cloak.

Mirror of Erised
One half of the Hogwarts Classrooms (set 4721) features the magical Mirror of Erised. The sticker on this magical LEGO piece shows Harry, wearing a black cloak (as left), with his parents, James and Lily Potter.

Harry's minifigure wears his characteristic determined expression.

This minifigure uses the same parts as the other 2001 variant (p.22).

Of the four Harry Potter minifigures released in 2001, two wore the Gryffindor uniform, one the Hogwarts uniform (p.18) and one was in casual clothes (p.10).

DATA FILE

SETS: 4706 Forbidden Corridor (2001), 4709 Hogwarts Castle (2001), 4721 Hogwarts Classrooms (2001)
PIECES: 5
ACCESSORIES: Cloak, brown wand, brown broom

Ron Weasley
─◆─ BOWL-HAIRED WIZARD ─◆─

For the 2004 update of the Ron minifigure, LEGO designers kept the young wizard's youthful, bowl-shaped hair piece and quirky grin. However, his uniform is slightly different from earlier versions, so that it matches those worn by Hermione and Harry.

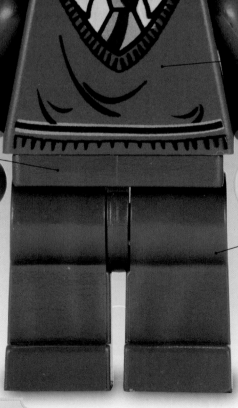

VARIANTS
─◆─

SETS: 4706 Forbidden Corridor (2001), 4709 Hogwarts Castle (2001), 4705 Snape's Class (2001), 4704 The Chamber of the Winged Keys (2001), 4730 Chamber of Secrets (2002)
PIECES: 5
ACCESSORIES: Light grey wand, cloak

Ron's flesh-coloured face still has freckles on his cheeks.

Ron's 2004 minifigure uniform keeps the Gryffindor colours, but does not have the house crest.

This minifigure of Ron is unique to the 2004 Hogwarts Castle set (4757).

The lighter grey of the earlier uniforms (above) has been replaced by a dark grey in the 2004 minifigure.

Did you know?
The 2004 minifigures were the last of Ron to feature his original face. A new design was released in 2005 (p.90).

DATA FILE
─◆─

SETS: 4751 Hogwarts Castle (2004)
PIECES: 4
ACCESSORIES: None

YEAR 1   Harry Potter and the Philosopher's Stone

The Fat Lady
—••— GUARD PORTRAIT OF GRYFFINDOR —••—

DATA FILE

SETS: 4709 Hogwarts
Castle (2001),
4722 Gryffindor
(2001)
PIECES: 1
ACCESSORIES: None

The 2004 variant features a more ornate frame and a different background (below).

The entrance to the Gryffindor common room is guarded by the Fat Lady portrait. Appearing in Hogwarts Castle (sets 4709 and 4757) and Gryffindor (set 4722), this LEGO piece swings open when the correct password is given.

In Gryffindor (set 4722), the picture frame is surrounded by orange bricks rather than these cream bricks from Hogwarts Castle (set 4709).

The Fat Lady wears a frilly pink dress.

Just like the early LEGO minifigures, the Fat Lady has yellow flesh tones.

VARIANTS

SETS: 4757 Hogwarts
Castle (2004)
PIECES: 1
ACCESSORIES: None

Did you know?
In the 2004 Hogwarts Castle (set 4757), the Fat Lady is missing from her portrait. Instead, the picture has been ripped and vandalised by a mysterious intruder.

Harry Potter and the Philosopher's Stone

YEAR **1**

25

Professor Snape
‑‑‑•⟶ POTIONS MASTER ⟶•‑‑‑

The stern Hogwarts Potions Master has appeared as five LEGO variants. Over time, his outfits and hairstyle have changed (p.105), and he was also the first LEGO minifigure to have glow-in-the-dark head and hands in 2001.

Professor Snape's face is printed with his characteristic sarcastically raised eyebrow.

(p.105)

VARIANTS

SETS: 4705 Snape's Class (2001), 4709 Hogwart's Castle (2001), 4733 The Duelling Club (2002)
PIECES: 5
ACCESSORIES: Spell book, magnifying glass, light grey wand, cloak

Professor Snape's 2004 outfit features a brighter purple frock coat than the 2001 variant.

Did you know?
One version of Snape's minifigure shows him dressed as Neville Longbottom's grandmother (p.71) – but in this case, it is actually a Boggart.

(p.71)

DATA FILE

SETS: 4751 Harry and the Marauder's Map (2004)
PIECES: 5
EQUIPMENT: Cloak

YEAR 1   Harry Potter and the Philosopher's Stone

Professor Quirrell
◆━ POSSESSED PROFESSOR ━◆

DATA FILE
◆━◆◆◆━◆

SETS: 4702 The Final Challenge (2001)
PIECES: 5
ACCESSORIES: Cloak, Philosopher's Stone

The minifigure of Professor Quirrell was the first to have a double-sided head – a feature that is now widely used across the LEGO universe. Quirrell taught Defence Against the Dark Arts during Harry's first year at Hogwarts, but is not all he seems to be...

Professor Quirrell's unique purple turban hides an unpleasant secret.

Professor Quirrell wears a purple jacket and scarf to match the colour of his exotic turban.

It's behind you!
Printed on the other side of Professor Quirrell's reversible head are the spooky features of Lord Voldemort, who has possessed the body of the Hogwarts professor.

Hidden behind the revolving mirror in The Final Challenge (set 4702) is the Philosopher's Stone itself, recreated in this ruby-red jewel piece.

Draco Malfoy
SLYTHERIN STUDENT

Draco's minifigure captures the Slytherin student's arrogance perfectly. His face is printed with a sneer to intimidate the other new students at Hogwarts School of Witchcraft and Wizardry.

VARIANTS

SETS: 4709 Hogwarts Castle (2001), 4711 Flying Lesson (2002), 4733 The Duelling Club (2002), 4735 Slytherin (2002)
PIECES: 5
ACCESSORIES: Remembrall, cloak, brown broom

The green and silver colours of Slytherin appear on the tie.

Draco's uniform has no crest, but the uniform worn by his 2001 variant (above) features the Slytherin crest.

This version of the Draco Malfoy minifigure is unique to Draco's Encounter with Buckbeak (set 4750), while the model of Buckbeak appears in another set: Sirius Black's Escape (set 4753).

DATA FILE

SETS: 4750 Draco's Encounter with Buckbeak (2004)
PIECES: 5
ACCESSORIES: Cloak

YEAR 1 Harry Potter and the Philosopher's Stone

Peeves
◄·◦─ PESKY POLTERGEIST ─◦·►

DATA FILE
▪◦◦━◦◦▪

SETS: 4709 Hogwarts
Castle (2001), 4705
Snape's Class (2001)
PIECES: 3
ACCESSORIES:
Cauldron and ladle

Haunting the corridors of Hogwarts Castle (set 4709), Peeves the Poltergeist is on the lookout for mischief and mayhem. The grey-bodied minifigure appears in two LEGO sets where he pops out unexpectedly from hiding places to spook passers-by.

Peeves' ghostly face is printed onto a light grey standard LEGO head.

Peeves' torso is printed with the ghostly markings of his jacket and shirt.

Peeves is hidden behind the door of a potions cabinet in Snape's Class (set 4705) and inside a hinged chimney breast in Hogwarts Castle (set 4709).

Tipping cauldron
In Snape's Class (set 4705), a cauldron and ladle are placed on top of a secret panel. When Peeves tips these over, the panel can slide back to reveal a hidden scroll.

Knight
SILVER STATUES

Guarding the corridors of Hogwarts, these Knight minifigures were created to protect the castle's many secrets. The silent warriors are armed with LEGO swords and conceal spooky objects within their armour.

VARIANTS

SETS: 4709
Hogwarts Castle
(2001)
PIECES: 6
ACCESSORIES:
Gryffindor
shield, sword

Beneath the helmet on this minifigure variant is a plain black head piece.

This helmet is formed from a single LEGO piece, while the helmet on the 2001 variant (above) is made from two pieces and covers the head of Peeves the Poltergeist (p.29).

The armour covering the chest has been given a pearl metallic sheen.

The Knight's hands are protected by dark bluish-grey armoured gloves.

Did you know?
In set 4842, the Knight hides Tom Riddle's diary. This is revealed when the Knight's plinth is spun around.

DATA FILE

SETS: 4842 Hogwarts
Castle (2010)
PIECES: 5
ACCESSORIES: Sword

YEAR
1
Harry Potter and the
Philosopher's Stone

Troll
➤➤ HOGWARTS INVADER ➤➤

DATA FILE
◆◆◆◆◆

SETS: 4712 Troll on the Loose (2002)
PIECES: 4
ACCESSORIES: Club, loincloth and vest

To create the fearsome troll that is released into Hogwarts by Professor Quirrell (p.27) in *Harry Potter and the Philosopher's Stone*, LEGO designers produced several unique parts. These include a terrifying sand blue head that is printed with red eyes and mouth and pointed fangs.

The large body comes in a single piece, with unposeable legs. The left arm is also fixed, but the right arm can swing back and forth.

The right hand is formed into a loop to hold a club, while the left hand is closed.

The troll comes with a unique cloth vest and a loincloth that is held up by an elastic waistband.

Mighty club
To create the troll's club, LEGO designers combined a light grey LEGO® *Star Wars*™ lightsaber part with a cone piece to form the long handle. This is topped off with a dark grey studded brick.

Harry Potter and the Philosopher's Stone

YEAR 1

Fluffy

THREE-HEADED DOG

Hogwarts' very own guard dog may be called "Fluffy", but there is nothing cute or cuddly about this hound. In the Forbidden Corridor (set 4706), this large LEGO figure guards the chamber leading to the Philosopher's Stone. His bark is worse than his bite, but few minifigures are brave enough to hang around and find out.

The Fluffy model is nearly twice as tall as a standard LEGO minifigure.

Did you know?

Harry puts Fluffy to sleep using a flute. In set 4706, this flute piece is printed with a magical owl.

Fluffy's three heads point in different directions, but all have the same expression.

Fluffy's heads are hinged so that the mouths can open and close.

DATA FILE

SETS: 4706 Forbidden Corridor (2001)
PIECES: 4
ACCESSORIES: Flute, treasure chest

The legs and lower part of the body come as a single piece and are unposeable.

YEAR 1   Harry Potter and the Philosopher's Stone

Chess Queen
❧❧ FACELESS RULER ❧❧

Checkmate
As the chess expert, it is Ron's task to defeat the Queen in a game of wizard chess. Once he has conquered the white army, he and Harry can progress to the Final Challenge (set 4702).

Having crept past the sleeping Fluffy, Harry must catch the flying keys and then face the challenge of the chess board in the Chamber of the Winged Keys (set 4704). The chess ruler is the Chess Queen, whose minifigure stands head and shoulders above Harry and Ron.

Unlike standard LEGO minifigures, the Chess Queen's head is a tall, faceless, barrel-shaped piece.

Did you know?
The Chess Queen's shiny silver crown is also found in the LEGO® Belville™ theme.

The moveable arms and hands are used to wield a white staff (above).

The Queen's unposeable legs are formed from a single sloped piece.

DATA FILE
━━━ ◆◆◆◆ ━━━
SETS: 4704 The Chamber of the Winged Keys (2001)
PIECES: 4
ACCESSORIES: White staff

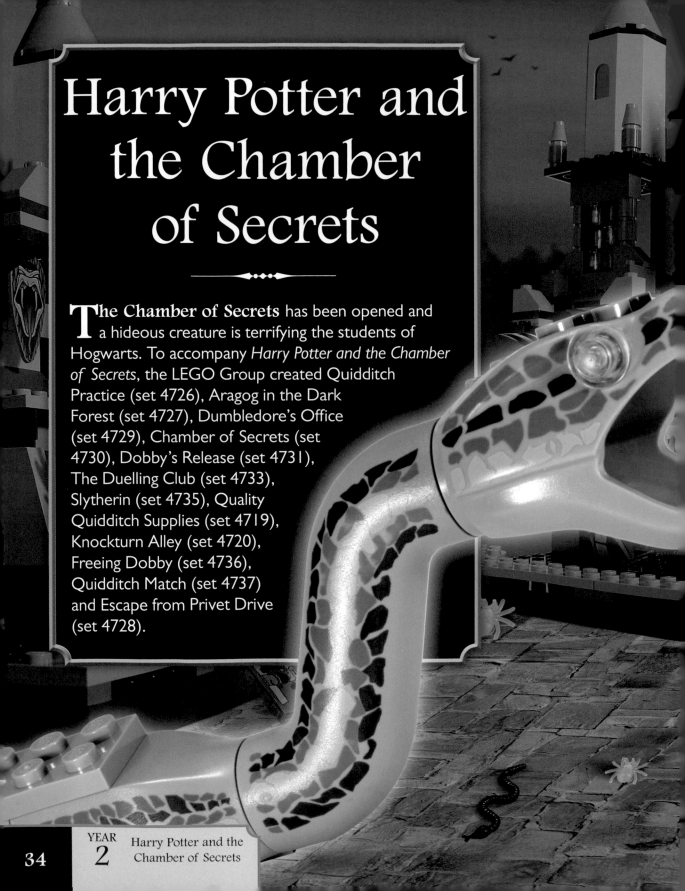

Harry Potter and the Chamber of Secrets

The Chamber of Secrets has been opened and a hideous creature is terrifying the students of Hogwarts. To accompany *Harry Potter and the Chamber of Secrets*, the LEGO Group created Quidditch Practice (set 4726), Aragog in the Dark Forest (set 4727), Dumbledore's Office (set 4729), Chamber of Secrets (set 4730), Dobby's Release (set 4731), The Duelling Club (set 4733), Slytherin (set 4735), Quality Quidditch Supplies (set 4719), Knockturn Alley (set 4720), Freeing Dobby (set 4736), Quidditch Match (set 4737) and Escape from Privet Drive (set 4728).

Harry Potter
TRAVELLING WIZARD

For his second year at Hogwarts, Harry's minifigure keeps many of the features used in earlier variants. Here, Harry wears casual clothes as he prepares to leave Aunt Petunia and Uncle Vernon's home in Privet Drive.

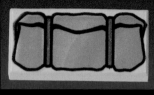

Ready to go
Escape from Privet Drive (set 4728) sees Harry ready to leave for Hogwarts with packed luggage and a bedroll, represented on this LEGO® tile. However, Harry's uncle has other ideas.

This minifigure of Harry in casual clothes is unique to set 4728.

Harry's torso is printed with a red and blue checked shirt over a blue t-shirt.

Even though he is wearing casual clothing, Harry's hips and legs are the same as those used in many of his Hogwarts uniforms.

Did you know?
Escape from Privet Drive (set 4728) features three letters from Hogwarts. These drop into Harry's room when the chimney stack on top of the house is turned.

DATA FILE

SETS: 4728 Escape from Privet Drive (2002)
PIECES: 4
ACCESSORIES: Letter tile, bedroll tile, black suitcase, light grey suitcase

Vernon Dursley
·◄—— OBSTINATE UNCLE ——►·

DATA FILE
·◄►·

SETS: 4728 Escape from
Privet Drive (2002)
PIECES: 4
ACCESSORIES: None

Vernon Dursley only appears
in one LEGO set: Escape from
Privet Drive (set 4728), where he
lives with his wife Petunia and their
son Dudley. LEGO designers have
managed to capture the character of
Harry's magic-hating uncle with his
scowling face and fierce moustache.

Uncle Vernon's hair
piece is the same shape
as the early Draco
Malfoy minifigures (p.28),
but a different colour.

Vernon's eyebrows
and moustache
match the colour
of his hair.

Vernon's unique torso
is printed with a brown
cardigan and blue
striped shirt.

Uncle Vernon is
the only member
of the Dursley family
to appear as a
minifigure in any
LEGO set.

Privet Drive
Number Four Privet Drive
is the scene of a dramatic
breakout when Ron arrives
to rescue Harry in set 4728.
The set even features a
bedroom window frame
that can be pulled out by
the Ford Anglia (p.17).

Harry Potter
❖⟩⟩ SHOPPING WIZARD ⟨⟨❖

For the first of Harry's visits to the mysterious shop of Borgin and Burkes in Knockturn Alley (set 4720), LEGO designers dressed Harry in a casual sand green and blue outfit. The shop's chimney breast is an entrance to the Floo Network, which Harry's minifigure can use to travel to Diagon Alley.

Spooky tiles
Knockturn Alley is the location of Borgin and Burkes, the Dark Arts shop. Inside are plenty of creepy artefacts. These include LEGO tiles decorated with a bag containing spiders and bones, and the Hand of Glory tile, featuring a shrivelled green hand.

This was the only minifigure of Harry released in 2003 and the last to feature yellow skin.

The combination of the sand green sweater and the blue trousers is unique to set 4720.

While Harry's torso is unique to this variant, the blue trousers are found on more than a thousand other LEGO minifigures.

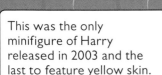

Did you know?
As well as the spider and bag tile and the Hand of Glory tile, Knockturn Alley (set 4720) comes with a very rare clear head piece printed with a floating brain.

DATA FILE
❖◆◆◆❖

SETS: 4720 Knockturn Alley (2003)
PIECES: 4
ACCESSORIES: Tile with spider and bag pattern

Dobby
LOYAL HOUSE~ELF

VARIANTS

SETS: 4731
Dobby's Release
(2002)
PIECES: 3
ACCESSORIES:
Sock tile

Dobby's 2010
minifigure head
has painted
green eyes.

This house~elf appears in Dobby's Release (set 4731) and Freeing Dobby (set 4736). The LEGO Group created this unique minifigure by crafting his head mould to accurately represent Dobby's unusual form, with bulging eyes and protruding ears. Both variants come with a LEGO sock tile, which Harry uses to trick Lucius Malfoy into releasing the house-elf.

Dobby's head is moulded with a rather forlorn expression due to his mistreatment by the cruel Lucius Malfoy.

DATA FILE

SETS: 4736 Freeing
Dobby (2010)
PIECES: 3
ACCESSORIES: Sock
tile, black book

Dobby's ragged outfit is held by a simple knot tied at the shoulder.

The torso is printed with Dobby's tattered outfit that is made from a dirty pillow case.

The later variant uses flesh-coloured head, arms and hands, rather than the tan pieces used in the earlier model.

Because Dobby is so small, his minifigure has short, unposeable legs, like the goblins (pp.12–13).

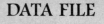

Lucius Malfoy
◆◆ PURE-BLOOD WIZARD ◆◆

Lucius **Malfoy** is an aristocratic wizard who believes that only those of pure blood should be allowed to practise magic. For his first appearance in LEGO Harry Potter, his minifigure appears alongside Dobby (p.39), the Malfoys' long-suffering house-elf.

All the variants of Lucius Malfoy have a sinister sneer printed on their faces.

This minifigure is dressed in a grey suit, while the 2003 variant has a black and red pinstripe jacket and no cloak (above).

The first Malfoy minifigure is unique to Dobby's Release (set 4731).

DATA FILE

SETS: 4731 Dobby's
Release (2002)
PIECES: 5
ACCESSORIES: Cloak,
black wand

Did you know?
Malfoy's hair is the same shape as Snape's (p.26) and Obi-Wan Kenobi's from LEGO®
Star Wars™.

YEAR
2
Harry Potter and the
Chamber of Secrets

Draco Malfoy

⊷ SNEERING WIZARD ⊷

Draco's 2003 minifigure features a slicked-down blond hair piece.

Harry's school nemesis, Draco Malfoy, has been recreated in eight LEGO minifigures. These show him in his Slytherin uniform, wearing Quidditch robes or, as here from set 4719, dressed in sinister black clothes.

Supply shop
Quality Quidditch Supplies (set 4719) stocks everything that a Quidditch player needs. This includes LEGO broomsticks, Quaffles, Bludgers, cloaks, flags and, of course, a Golden Snitch.

Like the minifigures of his father Lucius, Draco's face has a permanent sneer.

The outfit's details are picked out with grey highlights.

This minifigure is unique to Quality Quidditch Supplies (set 4719).

This is the only variant of Draco to show him not wearing a Slytherin uniform or a Quidditch outift.

DATA FILE

SETS: 4719 Quality Quidditch Supplies (2003)
PIECES: 4
ACCESSORIES: Earth orange broom, tile printed with parcel

Ginny Weasley
◄► YOUNGEST WEASLEY ◄►

The youngest member of the Weasley family, three variants of Ginny have appeared in three sets. This minifigure is in her first year at Hogwarts, so LEGO designers have given her a nervous expression, to show that she is worried about starting school.

Ginny's hair piece is the same as Professor Snape's (p.26) and Lucius Malfoy's (p.40), only this version is coloured earth orange.

This is the only variant of Ginny to feature a yellow head piece.

This Gryffindor tie has thicker golden stripes than later variants.

Like the rest of her family, Ginny is a Gryffindor, so her uniform features the lion crest.

Did you know?
The older variant of Ginny features a similar face to an older variant of Hermione from 2001 (p.20).

VARIANTS

SETS: 4841 Hogwarts Express (2010)
PIECES: 4
ACCESSORIES: Reddish-brown wand

DATA FILE
◄ ••••• ►
SETS: 4730 Chamber of Secrets (2002)
PIECES: 5
ACCESSORIES: Brown wand, cloak

Madame Hooch
◆→ FLYING INSTRUCTOR →◆

Brooms ready!
The other side of Hooch's reversible head shows the Quidditch flying instructor ready for action. Updated goggles are pulled tightly over her eyes and she now has a slight smile.

Madam Hooch is the flying instructor at Hogwarts, and she also referees Quidditch matches. LEGO designers have created two minifigures of the sporting staff member, both of which show her wearing a black suit and tie.

Madame Hooch now wears a black cloak while her 2002 variant wears a unique grey striped version (below).

Madame Hooch's 2010 face is painted with yellow eyes that have gold pupils, and she has the same hair piece as Ernie Prang (p.65).

Her black jacket bears a unique Hogwarts crest.

VARIANTS

SETS: 4726 Quidditch Practice (2002)
PIECES: 5
ACCESSORIES: Brown broom, Quidditch chest and balls

DATA FILE
◆→◆◆←◆

SETS: 4737 Quidditch Match (2010)
PIECES: 5
ACCESSORIES: Cloak, Quidditch trophy

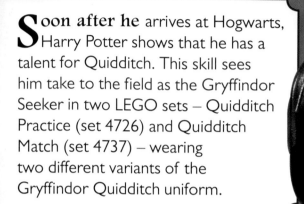

S oon after he arrives at Hogwarts, Harry Potter shows that he has a talent for Quidditch. This skill sees him take to the field as the Gryffindor Seeker in two LEGO sets – Quidditch Practice (set 4726) and Quidditch Match (set 4737) – wearing two different variants of the Gryffindor Quidditch uniform.

DATA FILE

SETS: 4737 Quidditch Match (2010), 852982 Magnet set
PIECES: 5
ACCESSORIES: Cloak, reddish-brown broom, Golden Snitch

The Gryffindor crest features on the updated uniform.

This minifigure has a reversible head. One face to smile when he wins and one to frown if he loses.

Harry's 2010 Quidditch uniform features thicker stripes to represent the woollen Quidditch jumpers.

VARIANTS

SETS: 4726 Quidditch Practice (2002)
PIECES: 5
ACCESSORIES: Brown broom, Golden Snitch

The 2010 variant wears a darker red uniform and gloves for protection.

Draco Malfoy
⟡ SLYTHERIN SEEKER ⟡

VARIANTS

SETS: 4726 Quidditch Practice (2002)
PIECES: 5
ACCESSORIES: Cloak, black broom

SETS: 4757 Hogwarts Castle (2004)
PIECES: 5
ACCESSORIES: Cloak, black broom

Draco Malfoy's feud with Harry Potter spills over onto the Quidditch pitch. Dressed in a Slytherin uniform, Draco faces Harry in both Quidditch Practice (set 4726) and Quidditch Match (set 4737).

Draco's head is reversible, featuring both a smirking and a worried face.

Draco wears the dark green and silver of the Slytherin Quidditch team.

The crest of Slytherin shows a coiled silver snake on a green shield.

The later Quidditch minifigure has white trousers, while the 2002 variant (above) has an all-green uniform.

DATA FILE

SETS: 4737 Quidditch Match (2010)
PIECES: 5
ACCESSORIES: Cloak, black broom

Marcus Flint
━━◄•❯ BEASTLY BEATER ❮•►━━

Marcus Flint is the captain of the Slytherin Quidditch team. When the LEGO Group created the Quidditch Match (set 4737), he was the perfect addition to help Draco Malfoy (p.45) and the Slytherin team try to clinch the Quidditch Cup.

Flint has the same shaped tousled hair piece as Oliver Wood (p.49).

DATA FILE
━━◄•◆•►━━

SETS: 4737 Quidditch Match (2010)
PIECES: 5
ACCESSORIES: Cloak, dark brown Beater's bat, black broom, helmet

Flint's smile shows that he is missing one of his teeth – perhaps through a Quidditch accident.

Player protection
Things can get rough in a Quidditch match, so LEGO designers have provided players with helmets. These can be placed on a minifigure's head once the hair piece has been removed.

As Beater, Flint wears brown gloves to grip his Beater's bat (a LEGO carrot piece coloured brown).

Quidditch captain Oliver Wood leads the Gryffindor team in set 4737, representing events from *Harry Potter and the Chamber of Secrets*. Wearing the scarlet and gold stripes of Gryffindor and protective Quidditch clothing, he is fully prepared to confront the challenge of the Slytherin team.

Quidditch Cup

LEGO designers have recreated the LEGO Quidditch cup with this metallic silver trophy. It comes with its own stand and is flanked by the flags of Gryffindor and Slytherin.

Wood's face is printed with a lop-sided grin, a dimple in his chin and a twinkle in his eyes.

Wood's minifigure is unique to Quidditch Match (set 4737).

From the neck down, Wood and Harry's minifigures (p.44) are the same, as they wear identical Quidditch uniforms.

DATA FILE

SETS: 4737 Quidditch Match (2010)
PIECES: 5
ACCESSORIES: Cloak, reddish-brown broom, helmet, Quidditch Cup trophy

Owls

Owls play an important role in the LEGO® Harry Potter™ theme, carrying letter tiles and parcels between wizards and their families. They also stand over many LEGO sets, such as Aragog in the Dark Forest (set 4727) and Graveyard Duel (set 4766), peering down on the minifigures below and adding to the spooky environment. LEGO designers have created two shapes of owl to appear in their sets. The more recent models feature added details and printed patterns to bring these distinctive pieces to life.

Bird of prey

For 2010, LEGO designers gave the familiar brown owl piece sharp angular eyebrows and fiercely staring yellow eyes. This variant has a printed tan chest with speckled feather detailing.

Harry's pet

This updated version of Hedwig is printed with feather patterns on her front as well as a black beak and yellow staring eyes. She appears in six sets, including Trolley (set 30110), which features just Hedwig and Harry.

Errol the owl

This light grey owl with mottled blue and brown feathers may represent the Weasleys' owl called Errol. This variant appears in five LEGO Harry Potter sets, including The Burrow (set 4840).

Black bird

The original owl piece has a rounded head and eyes. This black variant is very common, appearing in nine LEGO sets, of which eight are from the LEGO Harry Potter theme.

Town and country

The dark grey variant of the LEGO owl appears in four sets: Aragog in the Dark Forest (set 4727), Gryffindor (set 4722), Hogwarts Castle (set 4709) and Knockturn Alley (set 4720).

Snowy owl

The first version of Harry's white owl Hedwig is the most common owl piece. It can be found in eleven LEGO Harry Potter sets, including three versions of Hogwarts Castle (sets 4709, 4757 and 5378).

At the shops

This light grey owl appears in four LEGO sets in total, two from Harry Potter: Chamber of Secrets (set 4730) and Diagon Alley Shops (set 4723). The other two sets are from the LEGO® Belville™ theme.

Forest dweller

The tan variant of the owl appears perched above Hagrid's Hut (set 4707), looking down on Draco's Encounter with Buckbeak (set 4750) and in the eerie trees in Aragog in the Dark Forest (set 4727).

Rare visitor

The brown and reddish-brown variants are the rarest of the owls, appearing in just three sets between them. The reddish-brown owl is only found in Motorised Hogwarts Express (set 10132), where Harry is travelling to school.

Mandrake
SCREAMING PLANT

The screaming Mandrake plants are kept in a greenhouse in the grounds of Hogwarts Castle (set 5378). Students learn to handle these dangerous plants under the guidance of Professor Sprout (p.134).

DATA FILE

SETS: 5378 Hogwarts Castle (2007)
PIECES: 2
ACCESSORIES: Reddish-brown barrel

The unique screaming Mandrake face is printed on a standard LEGO head piece.

Large leaves — also found on a multitude of other LEGO plants — sit on top of the Mandrake's head.

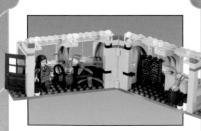

The greenhouse
Part of Hogwarts Castle (set 5378), the greenhouse is where the pupils are taught to re-pot the Mandrake plant. The screams from a fully grown Mandrake can kill, so they must be handled with care.

Did you know?
Hogwarts Castle (set 5378) has two Mandrake plants, and both can be pulled out of their barrels.

A classic brown barrel piece fits the Mandrake snugly — and stops it from screaming.

Professor Lockhart
⇢ WELL-DRESSED PROFESSOR ⇢

Flipping spells
The Duelling Club (set 4733) features a special platform that flips minifigures when they are hit by a spell. The set also has two banners featuring the Hogwarts crest.

Famed for his heroic stories about defeating dangerous creatures, Professor Lockhart seems the ideal choice to head the Duelling Club (set 4733). And with his bright green clothes, his minifigure stands out from the rest of the Hogwarts staff.

Lockhart's minifigures come with thick blond hair and a permanent wide grin.

Emerald cloaks are worn by two other LEGO Harry Potter minifigures – Draco Malfoy (p.45) and Professor McGonagall (p.106).

The emerald waistcoat is printed with an elaborate gold design.

Did you know?
The Duelling Club (set 4733) contains a model of the snake conjured up by Draco Malfoy during his duel with Harry Potter.

DATA FILE
SETS: 4733 The Duelling Club (2002)
PIECES: 5
ACCESSORIES: Cloak, tan wand

Gregory Goyle
⊷•• SLYTHERIN INFILTRATOR ••⊶

This minifigure is actually Harry, in disguise and undertaking a dangerous mission to spy on Draco Malfoy. To do so, he has to drink the revolting Polyjuice Potion and walk into Slytherin (set 4735), without revealing his true identity.

Goyle's hair piece is found on several other LEGO minifigures, including Draco Malfoy (p.28), and Neville Longbottom (p.72).

Disguised Harry
Polyjuice Potion allows a wizard to take on another person's form. Harry now resembles Malfoy's sidekick Goyle – but the effects don't last long. Turn his head around and Harry's familiar expression is revealed!

All three minifigures that come with set 4735, including Draco, use the same torso and leg pieces.

Did you know?
Goyle's updated minifigure (p.138) uses the same flat-topped hair piece as Vincent Crabbe.

DATA FILE
⊷•••◆•••⊶

SETS: 4735 Slytherin (2002)
PIECES: 5
ACCESSORIES: Cloak, brown wand

YEAR **2** Harry Potter and the Chamber of Secrets

Vincent Crabbe
— UNDERCOVER GRYFFINDOR —

Disguised Ron
Ron's grinning features, complete with orange eyebrows, appear on the reverse side of the head. The Gryffindor pupil has taken Polyjuice Potion to disguise himself as Malfoy's crony, Vincent Crabbe.

All is not what it seems with this minifigure. A simple turn of his reversible head reveals the smiling features of Ron Weasley, who is accompanying Harry on his secret mission into set 4735.

As with all minifigures from Slytherin house, Crabbe's face is printed with a stern scowl.

As well as the current members of Slytherin house, this torso is used for the minifigure of Tom Riddle (p.59).

The starred cloak appears with ten LEGO Harry Potter minifigures, including Crabbe and Goyle.

DATA FILE
SETS: 4735 Slytherin (2002)
PIECES: 5
ACCESSORIES: Cloak, brown wand

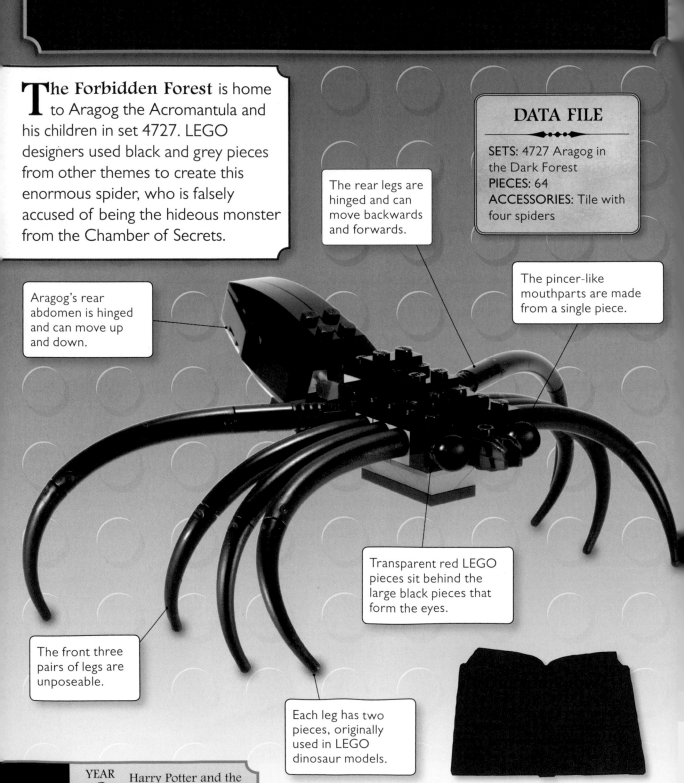

The Forbidden Forest is home to Aragog the Acromantula and his children in set 4727. LEGO designers used black and grey pieces from other themes to create this enormous spider, who is falsely accused of being the hideous monster from the Chamber of Secrets.

The rear legs are hinged and can move backwards and forwards.

DATA FILE

SETS: 4727 Aragog in the Dark Forest
PIECES: 64
ACCESSORIES: Tile with four spiders

The pincer-like mouthparts are made from a single piece.

Aragog's rear abdomen is hinged and can move up and down.

Transparent red LEGO pieces sit behind the large black pieces that form the eyes.

The front three pairs of legs are unposeable.

Each leg has two pieces, originally used in LEGO dinosaur models.

Aragog
➤➤ HAIRY ARACHNID ➤➤

Spider children
Hagrid's Hut (set 4738) comes with three small spiders that represent Aragog's children. Other animals featured include a rat, two owls and Norbert, the baby dragon.

Aragog's updated abdomen is printed with large black hairs.

The 2010 version of Hagrid's Hut (4738) features a more complicated model of Aragog. The new version is fully poseable and has extra details, including angry eyes, a hairy body and eight moveable legs so that the giant spider can roam through the Forbidden Forest.

Aragog's face now features green printed eyes.

The mouth parts are the horn pieces used in LEGO® Viking helmets.

DATA FILE
➤➤✦➤➤

SETS: 4738 Hagrid's Hut (2010)
PIECES: 52
ACCESSORIES: Black baby spiders

The legs for the 2010 model are made from LEGO Ninja sword pieces.

Did you know?
Most spiders have four pairs of eyes, but this minifigure of Aragog only has three pairs.

Harry Potter
➤• WIZARD IN THE WOODS •➤

When Hogwarts minifigures are mysteriously attacked, Harry ventures deep into the Forbidden Forest to investigate. Wearing a casual outfit and equipped with his trusty wand, he follows the LEGO spiders into the woods and encounters Aragog (pp.54–55).

Magic wands
As well as appearing in the LEGO Harry Potter theme as a wizard's wand, this piece is used in the LEGO *Star Wars* theme as a lightsaber blade and a whole host of other roles in more than 500 different sets right across the LEGO universe.

Even though he is venturing into the scary Forbidden Forest, Harry still has a determined smile printed on his face.

Harry's unique torso shows him wearing a dark blue zip-up jacket and a pale blue collared shirt.

These light grey leg pieces are found on 129 minifigures across the LEGO universe.

DATA FILE
➤••••➤

SETS: 4727 Aragog in the Dark Forest (2002)
PIECES: 4
ACCESSORIES: Brown wand

Did you know?
Three Harry minifigures were released in 2002, and none show him wearing his uniform.

Ron Weasley
⟶• ARACHNOPHOBE WIZARD •⟵

DATA FILE

SETS: 4727 Aragog in the Dark Forest (2002)
PIECES: 4
ACCESSORIES: Light grey wand

Creeping into the Forbidden Forest alongside Harry in set 4727, Ron needs to take care where he steps. One false move and he could spring Aragog's trap exposing the student wizard to his greatest fear – spiders! Luckily for him, Aragog isn't hungry, but the same can't be said for his children!

Although this was the last Ron minifigure to feature a yellow head and hands, he kept his bowl-shaped hair piece until 2007.

Ron's minifigure comes with a unique torso showing him dressed in casual clothes of a zip-up plaid jacket and dark grey trousers.

Spider children
Set 4727 comes with this unique tile printed with four coloured spiders. These represent Aragog's children. Other LEGO animals featured in the set include a black spider piece and two owls: one tan, one grey.

This is the only minifigure of Ron to be released in 2002.

Professor Lockhart
— CELEBRITY PROFESSOR —

Even when he has to face the terrifying Basilisk (p.60) in the Chamber of Secrets (set 4730), LEGO designers have made sure that Professor Lockhart is well dressed and flashing his trademark grin. The egotistical professor looks good, but his fashionable outfit covers a cowardly heart.

Did you know?
Lockhart, Harry and Ron enter the Chamber of Secrets (set 4730) through a trapdoor in the girls' bathroom, which sends them sliding down a ramp of smooth LEGO tiles.

Lockhart's hair piece is the same shape as the one worn by Professor Lupin (p.67)

Just like his other minifigure (p.51), Lockhart is shown wearing a brightly coloured suit with an ornate waistcoat.

The sand red hips and legs and the printed torso are unique to this minifigure of Lockhart.

DATA FILE

SETS: 4730 Chamber of Secrets (2002)
PIECES: 5
ACCESSORIES: Cloak, dark orange wand

Tom Riddle
⟶ FUTURE DARK LORD ⟶

Tom's diary
The hinged LEGO tile that is Tom Riddle's ink-splattered diary is found in Chamber of Secrets (set 4730) and Dobby's Release (set 4731). It can be opened just like a real book.

Brought back to life briefly as part of the Chamber of Secrets (set 4730), Tom Riddle commands the Basilisk (p.60) to attack Harry Potter. Riddle's minifigure comes with his diary. This tatty book is also a Horcrux – an object in which he has hidden a piece of his soul.

At first glance you might mistake this minifigure for Harry, as they share the same hair piece. But Tom's sinister expression reveals his evil nature.

During his time at Hogwarts, Riddle was a member of Slytherin, so he wears the green and silver uniform.

While the other student minifigures in set 4730 wear starred cloaks, Riddle's is plain black.

DATA FILE
⟶⟵

SETS: 4730 Chamber of Secrets (2002)
PIECES: 5
ACCESSORIES: Cloak, diary

Basilisk
SUBTERRANEAN SNAKE

Deep beneath the floors of Hogwarts slithers the enormous Basilisk. LEGO designers have captured the full horror of this massive monster as part of the Chamber of Secrets (set 4730). The beast has sinister yellow eyes and razor-sharp, venomous fangs.

The Basilisk's eyes are transparent yellow pieces.

The neck and tail parts are articulated and poseable.

DATA FILE

SETS: 4730 Chamber of Secrets (2002)
PIECES: 13
ACCESSORIES: None

The fierce fang pieces glow in the dark.

The Basilisk's body parts are printed with green scales.

The central body piece has LEGO studs to fix it to the base of the Chamber of Secrets (set 4730).

Did you know?
Basilisk fangs are LEGO knife pieces, so they can be pulled out and used to eventually destroy Horcruxes.

Grand entrance
In The Chamber of Secrets (set 4730), the Basilisk makes its entrance through the hinged doors of the statue of the founder of Slytherin house. Flaming torches stand on either side to add to the ominous atmosphere.

Fawkes
◄— DUMBLEDORE'S PHOENIX —►

A LEGO stud forms the phoenix's crest.

The wings have a moulded feather texture.

Dumbledore's phoenix, Fawkes, is only found in the Chamber of Secrets (set 4730). This magical bird plays a key role in the set: delivering the sword of Gryffindor to Harry and healing his Basilisk bite with phoenix tears.

Fawkes is made from a single LEGO piece.

DATA FILE
SETS: 4730 Chamber of Secrets (2002)
PIECES: 1
ACCESSORIES: Black Sorting Hat, sword of Gryffindor

The tail section has small handles that a LEGO minifigure can hold on to.

Magical sword
The sword of Gryffindor, which Harry uses to slay the Basilisk, appears in two Harry Potter LEGO sets: The Chamber of Secrets (set 4730) and Hogwarts Castle (set 4842).

The crimson-coloured piece is the first phoenix ever made by the LEGO Group.

Harry Potter and the Prisoner of Azkaban

Sirius Black has escaped the wizards' prison of Azkaban and is on a mission. The LEGO Group released 11 sets for Harry's dramatic third year at Hogwarts: Draco's Encounter with Buckbeak (set 4750), Harry and the Marauder's Map (set 4751), Professor Lupin's Classroom (set 4752), Sirius Black's Escape (set 4753), Hagrid's Hut (set 4754), Knight Bus (set 4755), Shrieking Shack (set 4756), Hogwarts Castle (set 4757), Hogwarts Express (set 4758), Motorised Hogwarts Express (set 10132) and The Knight Bus (set 4866).

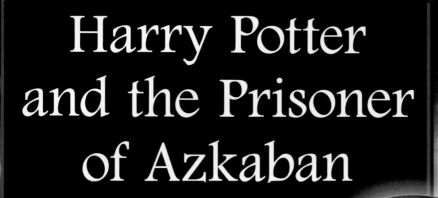

4756 Shrieking Shack (2004)

Stan Shunpike
KNIGHT BUS CONDUCTOR

The **Knight Bus** transports wizards from place to place, and is used to rescue Harry when he is stranded at the beginning of *Harry Potter and the Prisoner of Azkaban*. The LEGO Group has created two versions of the Bus, in 2004 (set 4755) and 2011 (set 4866), and Stan has appeared in both.

Stan's 2011 minifigure has cheek lines and dimples painted on his face, while the 2004 minifigure has strands of hair.

Stan is the ticket collector, or conductor, on the Knight Bus and he carries a ticket machine around his chest.

Stan also has a satchel strap running diagonally across his torso.

Stan's second figure is unique to set 4866.

DATA FILE

SETS: 4866 The Knight Bus (2011)
PIECES: 4
ACCESSORIES: None

Did you know?
Stan was the first LEGO® minifigure to be made almost entirely out of purple pieces.

YEAR 3 | Harry Potter and the Prisoner of Azkaban

Ernie Prang
✦✦ KNIGHT BUS DRIVER ✦✦

DATA FILE

SETS: 4866 The Knight Bus (2011)
PIECES: 4
ACCESSORIES: Shrunken head

Ernie Prang, or "Ern" as Stan Shunpike calls him, is the driver of the Knight Bus. Along with a shrunken head and Stan to keep him company, the cab of Ernie's Knight Bus (set 4866) also has a gear lever and steering wheel for him to operate.

Ernie's minifigure has the same hair piece as Madam Hooch (p.43).

The head is printed with a grey beard and thick glasses that are held together with sticky tape.

Ernie's unique torso is printed with a grey shirt, black tie and undone knitted waistcoat.

Ernie's minifigure is exclusive to set 4866.

Shrunken head
For the 2011 version of the Knight Bus (set 4866), LEGO designers used a sand green round piece printed with the shrunken head's features. In set 4755, the head was printed on the windscreen.

Dementor

◄◄ FLYING PRISON GUARDS ►►

The Dementors act as guards of Azkaban prison and also hunt down escaped prisoners. LEGO designers have created two versions of these spooky figures. The second grey variant came with an inverted LEGO dish that could be attached to the bottom to keep the Dementor upright.

The other side
The reverse side of the 2011 Dementor head is almost completely blank, with the gaping hole closed and just a few facial crease lines.

The hood is the same as the one worn by Lucius Malfoy as a Death Eater (p.132).

Dementors have large gaping mouths through which they try to suck out a person's soul.

Underneath the cloak a Dementor has the same torso used on the skeletons (pp.94–95).

VARIANTS
◆◆◆◆
SETS: 4757 Hogwarts Castle (2004), 4758 Hogwarts Express (2004), 10132 Motorised Hogwarts Express (2004), 4753 Sirius Black's Escape (2004)
PIECES: 7
ACCESSORIES: Cloak

DATA FILE
◆◆◆◆
SETS: 4842 Hogwarts Castle (2010), 4867 Hogwarts (2011)
PIECES: 8
ACCESSORIES: Cloak

YEAR **3**   Harry Potter and the Prisoner of Azkaban

Professor Lupin
➤➤ WEREWOLF WIZARD ➤➤

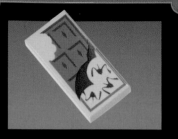

Chocolate treat
To represent the bar of chocolate that Lupin hands Harry to ward off the bad effects of the Dementors, LEGO designers have made this tile to go with the minifigure.

When it is a full moon, kindly Professor Lupin transforms into a snarling werewolf. To show this, LEGO designers have created two versions of his 2004 minifigure. One shows the professor ready to teach Defence Against the Dark Arts classes, while the other comes with a werewolf head piece.

Lupin's face has scratch marks from his adventures as a werewolf.

Lupin's torso is painted with the torn and tatty suit he wears when he first arrives at Hogwarts.

DATA FILE
SETS: 4758 Hogwarts Express (2004), 10132 Motorised Hogwarts Express (2004), 4752 Professor Lupin's Classroom (2004)
PIECES: 5
ACCESSORIES: Dark orange wand, chocolate tile, cloak

VARIANTS

SETS: 4756 Shrieking Shack (2004)
PIECES: 5
ACCESSORIES: Cloak, werewolf head

Harry Potter and the Prisoner of Azkaban

Harry Potter
— THE BOY WIZARD —

On board the Hogwarts Express (set 4758) to start his third year at school, Harry's minifigure wears plain casual clothes. He only appears dressed like this on one other occasion – in the Shrieking Shack (set 4756).

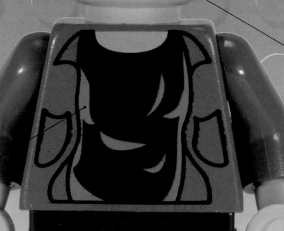

Did you know?
Harry is the only figure in set 4756 who can't transform into an animal – unlike Lupin, Sirius Black, and Peter Pettigrew.

The 2004 Harry Potter minifigures were the first to feature flesh-coloured heads and hands. Before then, they had been yellow.

Harry's torso, featuring a grey, unbuttoned shirt and a red shirt, also appears in set 4756.

On the Hogwarts Express (set 4758) Harry wears blue trousers, but changes to dark tan when he visits the Shrieking Shack (set 4756).

YEAR 3 Harry Potter and the Prisoner of Azkaban

Ron Weasley
FAITHFUL FRIEND

Ron's early minifigures come with a bowl-shaped hair piece (p.17).

Ron accompanies Harry on the Hogwarts Express (set 4758) as they travel back to school. He is also casually dressed and carrying a wand, unaware that they are about to encounter a Dementor for the first time.

Scabbers
Ron inherits a pet rat called Scabbers from his family. In sets 4758 and 10132 he appears as a standard LEGO rat. For the Shrieking Shack (set 4756), however, he is shown in a upright position, perhaps hinting at his real human form (p.98).

This expression is found not only on Ron's minifigure, but also on the reverse side of Vincent Crabbe's head – when Ron is disguised as the Slytherin student (p.53).

Ron's torso, with open shirt and green and pink striped sweater, only appears in the two 2004 train sets.

DATA FILE

SETS: 4758 Hogwarts Express (2004), 10132 Motorised Hogwarts Express (2004)
PIECES: 4
ACCESSORIES: Light bluish-grey wand

Neville Longbottom
NERVOUS GRYFFINDOR

For the first of his two minifigures, LEGO designers chose to show Neville at an important stage of his education – confronting and dealing with his worst fear inside Professor Lupin's Classroom (set 4752).

Neville's 2011 version (p.135) has a broader smile and more pronounced eyebrows than this minifigure.

Lupin's classroom
Professor Lupin's classroom is filled with magical props, including potion bottles, three LEGO skulls, spell books and a giant spider's web.

Neville has the same torso and legs as the other 2004 Gryffindor minifigures, Harry and Ron.

DATA FILE

SETS: 4752 Professor Lupin's Classroom (2004)
PIECES: 5
ACCESSORIES: Cloak, black wand

YEAR **3** Harry Potter and the Prisoner of Azkaban

Boggart
SHAPE~SHIFTER

DATA FILE

SETS: 4752 Professor Lupin's Classroom (2004)
PIECES: 4
ACCESSORIES: None

As a shape~shifter, a Boggart can take any form, but usually transforms itself into the thing that a person fears the most. When Neville Longbottom confronts one in Professor Lupin's Classroom (set 4752), it turns into Snape. To counter its effects, Neville charms the Boggart minifigure so that it is wearing his grandmother's clothes.

This is the last of Snape's minifigures with a glow-in-the-dark head.

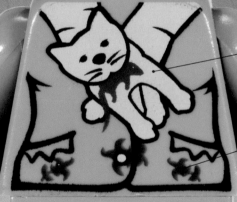

The Boggart's unique sand green torso is printed with Neville's grandmother's cardigan and cat-shaped scarf.

The Boggart's cardigan is decorated with green flower patterns.

The Boggart has light-bluish grey hands.

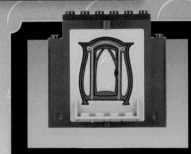

Spinning door
The Boggart is hidden inside a mirrored cupboard, which stands in one corner of Professor Lupin's Classroom (set 4752). The door spins round to release the shape-shifting creature.

Harry Potter
THIRD-YEAR WIZARD

For the release of *Harry Potter and the Prisoner of Azkaban*, the LEGO Group created six minifigures of Harry. Three of them are in casual clothing, with the others in his Gryffindor uniform. Dressed for action, the young wizard is ready for the arrival of the escaped convict Sirius Black (p.78).

DATA FILE
SETS: 4757 Hogwarts Castle (2004)
PIECES: 4
ACCESSORIES: Black wand

The 2007 variant of this minifigure (p.112) has the same torso and legs as this 2004 variant, but with a redesigned face.

The 2004 Harry minifigures were the last to feature this face, with one eyebrow raised in a quizzical fashion.

VARIANTS

SETS: 4753 Sirius Black's Escape (2004)
PIECES: 5
ACCESSORIES: Cloak, black wand

SETS: 4751 Harry and the Marauder's Map (2004)
PIECES: 5
ACCESSORIES: Cloak, black wand with *Lumos* spell

The three uniformed minifigures of Harry released in 2004 have the same torso and legs, but two come with cloaks: one black, one violet (left).

Marauder's Map Statue
➤➤ SILENT SENTRY ➤➤

Armed with the Marauder's Map in set 4751, Harry is able to see every inch of Hogwarts castle and the locations of all the minifigures in it. He can also see the whereabouts of secret passages, but to enter one of them, he has to get past this looming minifigure statue.

Like the Chess Queen (p.33), the statue's head piece is faceless.

The statue's dark bluish-grey torso and legs are printed with a flowing robe.

The statue's legs are formed from a single sloped piece, so they are unposeable, like any statue.

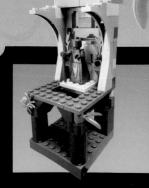

Secret passage
As part of Harry and the Marauder's Map (set 4751), the statue guards a secret passage. This leads Harry to Honeydukes sweet shop in *Harry Potter and the Prisoner of Azkaban*.

DATA FILE
➤•◆•➤

SETS: 4751 Harry and the Marauder's Map (2004)
PIECES: 3
ACCESSORIES: Marauder's Map, dark bluish-grey wand

Snakes, frogs and dragons

The magical world of Harry Potter is filled with strange and exotic creatures and many of them have found their way into the LEGO® sets. This marvellous menagerie includes standard LEGO animals, such as snakes and frogs, as well as mythical figures, such as dragons.

Gateposts

This black version of the dragon slots onto the studs found on top of the graveyard gateposts in set 4766.

Baby Norbert

This dark green model of Norbert appears in the 2010 version of Hagrid's Hut (set 4738). The model has a pointed head with a wide mouth and spines running down its back.

Hagrid's pet

This variant of the baby dragon Norbert appears in the 2001 version of Hagrid's Hut (set 4707). The sand-green variant of newborn Norbert the Norwegian Ridgeback is unique to this set and to the LEGO Harry Potter theme.

Stone frog
This dark bluish-grey variant frog piece forms part of an unusual headstone in the Graveyard Duel (set 4766).

Green frog
This green frog variant is part of eight LEGO Harry Potter sets, including Snape's Classroom (set 4705).

Chocolate frog
Having also appeared in the LEGO® Belville™ theme, the frog piece can be found in some 37 sets. This variant is coloured brown because it represents the edible chocolate frogs found on the Hogwarts Express (set 4841) and in Diagon Alley (set 10217).

Rare reptile
This red snake only appears in one Harry Potter set: Graveyard Duel (set 4766).

Snake-filled Chamber
The Chamber of Secrets (set 4730) has no fewer than five black snakes.

Nagini
Slithering through the corridors during the battle of Hogwarts (set 4867), this green snake variant represents Lord Voldemort's snake companion, Nagini. This gigantic reptile is a Horcrux and contains a piece of the Dark Lord's soul. Fortunately Neville Longbottom (p.135) is on hand to kill the snake so that Harry can defeat Voldemort.

Hermione Granger
TIME TRAVELLER

This **Hermione** minifigure is exclusive to Hogwarts Castle (set 4757). Her grey Gryffindor uniform is printed with a magical addition, the Time-Turner. Hermione uses this to give herself more time to study and also to save the Hippogriff, Buckbeak (p.79).

DATA FILE

SETS: 4757 Hogwarts Castle (2004)
PIECES: 4
ACCESSORIES: Dark bluish-grey wand

This minifigure uses the same printed face from earlier yellow figures (p.16).

The Gryffindor uniform and the Time-Turner are found printed on a cloaked variant of Hermione in set 4754 (below, left).

Hermione's uniform features the scarlet and gold stripes of her house, but without the Gryffindor crest.

VARIANTS

SETS: 4754 Hagrid's Hut (2004)
PIECES: 5
ACCESSORIES: Dark bluish-grey wand, cloak

Did you know?
Hogwarts Castle (set 4757) has a mechanism that connects to the clock face to open the entrance.

YEAR
3
Harry Potter and the Prisoner of Azkaban

Professor Trelawney
— ▪◆▪ DIVINATION TEACHER ▪◆▪ —

Did you know?
Professor Trelawney's Divination classroom in the roof of Hogwarts Castle (set 4757) comes with cups for reading tea leaves and a crystal ball containing a LEGO skull!

Professor Trelawney believes she has powerful abilities to see the future. Her classroom at Hogwarts Castle (set 4757) contains all the equipment she needs for Divination, and her minifigure comes with a unique outfit to match her character.

Professor Trelawney's face is printed with thick glasses and dimples on either side of her mouth.

Professor Trelawney is the only witch or wizard minifigure to wear a pink hat.

Trelawney's outfit is completed by a purple shawl, beaded belt and matching necklace.

DATA FILE
— ▪◆▪ —

SETS: 4757 Hogwarts Castle (2004)
PIECES: 4
ACCESSORIES: None

The bottom of her dress is formed from a single piece, which is unposeable.

The shimmering effect of the sequins that decorate Professor Trelawney's dress is recreated in the flowing pattern printed on the torso and leg pieces.

Sirius Black
ESCAPED CONVICT

H ogwarts is placed on high alert when Sirius Black escapes from Azkaban prison. Sirius appears in six LEGO sets in total, but not all of them as a minifigure. His other appearances include a wanted poster (p.133), a face in the flickering flames of a fire (right) and as a sinister dog that is his Animagus form (below).

In the fire
Black communicates with his godson Harry at Hogwarts by appearing to him within the fireplace in the Gryffindor common room. LEGO designers have portrayed this event in two later versions of Hogwarts (sets 5378 and 4842).

Black's face is printed with the unshaven face and stern expression of an escaped prisoner.

Black wears the tattered uniform of Azkaban, the wizard's prison.

VARIANTS

SETS: 4755 Knight Bus (2004)
PIECES: 1
ACCESSORIES: None

DATA FILE

SETS: 4756 Shrieking Shack (2004), 4753 Sirius Black's Escape (2004)
PIECES: 4
ACCESSORIES: None

YEAR
3
Harry Potter and the Prisoner of Azkaban

Buckbeak

⊷ RESCUED HIPPOGRIFF ⊶

DATA FILE

SETS: 4750 Draco's Encounter with Buckbeak (2004), 4753 Sirius Black's Escape (2004)
PIECES: 3
ACCESSORIES: None

The LEGO Group created the proud Hippogriff Buckbeak for two Harry Potter sets. In Draco's Encounter with Buckbeak (set 4750), the magical creature attacks the arrogant Slytherin student, while in Sirius Black's Escape (set 4753), he carries the escaped convict to safety on his back.

Four LEGO studs on Buckbeak's back allow minifigures to ride the Hippogriff.

A Hippogriff's body is half-horse, half-eagle.

Buckbeak's head is hinged so that the Hippogriff can bow as a sign of respect.

Did you know?

Buckbeak's wings are also found on the skeleton above Tom Riddle's tomb in Graveyard Duel (set 4766).

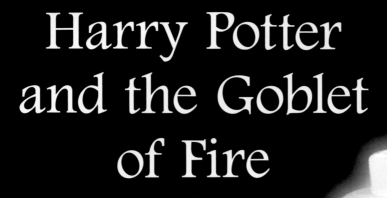

Harry Potter and the Goblet of Fire

Harry's fourth year at Hogwarts sees him compete in the Triwizard Tournament and battle Voldemort himself. To recreate these scenes, four LEGO® sets were released based on the movie *Harry Potter and the Goblet of Fire*: The Durmstrang Ship (set 4768), Harry and the Hungarian Horntail (set 4767), Rescue from the Merpeople (set 4762) and Graveyard Duel (set 4766).

YEAR 4   Harry Potter and the Goblet of Fire

4766 Graveyard Duel (2005)

Professor Karkaroff
— ·•· DURMSTRANG HEADMASTER ·•· —

The Durmstrang Ship (set 4768) carries the students from Durmstrang Institute to take part in the Triwizard Tournament. In charge of this party is the grim-faced Headmaster, Professor Igor Karkaroff. His fierce expression shows he wants his school to win!

Karkaroff wears a large, fur-like LEGO hat to keep his head warm.

The Professor's face is printed with a sneering grimace and a goatee beard.

The torso is printed with a fur-lined jacket that is fastened with tooth-shaped toggles.

Sailor's map
The Durmstrang Ship (set 4768) comes with a full complement of nautical equipment. This includes a sailing map, which is also found in another 23 sea-based LEGO sets.

Durmstrang Institute lies in the cold north, so its staff and pupils must dress warmly to keep out the chill.

DATA FILE
— ·•·•·•· —

SETS: 4768 The Durmstrang Ship (2005)
PIECES: 4
ACCESSORIES: Reddish-brown wand, nautical map tile

YEAR 4 — Harry Potter and the Goblet of Fire

Viktor Krum
DURMSTRANG CHAMPION

Krum's head is also found in the LEGO® Indiana Jones™ theme and on a commentator from Grand Prix Race (set 8161).

Arriving on the Durmstrang Ship (set 4768) with Professor Karkaroff is the school champion, Viktor Krum. The stern expression on this minifigure's face shows that he is totally focussed on taking part in the three tasks ahead of him.

Did you know?
The top deck of the Durmstrang Ship opens up to reveal a cosy cabin with hinged double-doors, a desk, ink pot, a cauldron and a shelf holding a blue goblet.

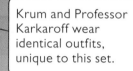

Krum and Professor Karkaroff wear identical outfits, unique to this set.

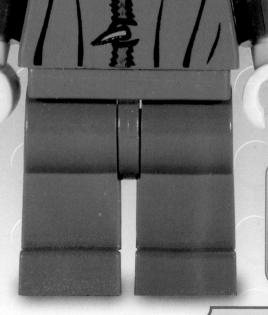

Finding the way
The Durmstrang sailors need the right equipment to navigate beyond their northern waters. As well as maps and charts (p.84), set 4768 features a bluish-grey sextant piece that is found in another 29 LEGO sets.

DATA FILE

SETS: 4768 The Durmstrang Ship (2005)
PIECES: 4
ACCESSORIES: Sextant

Harry Potter
TRIWIZARD CHAMPION

The **Triwizard** Tournament sees champions from three magic schools compete in three difficult tasks. The first of these is to retrieve a golden egg that is guarded by a dragon. Harry faces the fiercest dragon of them all – the Hungarian Horntail – so LEGO designers dressed him in a special uniform.

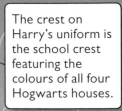

Dragon's egg
The LEGO golden egg has a small magnetic piece on one side. LEGO designers solved the problem of picking up the round egg by giving Harry a magnetic handle that he could hold in his hand.

Harry's surname is printed on his chest and on the back of the torso.

The crest on Harry's uniform is the school crest featuring the colours of all four Hogwarts houses.

Harry's Tournament uniform features tears and scrapes from the various Triwizard tasks.

Did you know?
Set 4767 features a catapult that shoots a broom to Harry, so that he can avoid the dragon.

DATA FILE
------◆◆◆◆------
SETS: 4767 Harry and the Hungarian Horntail (2005)
PIECES: 4
ACCESSORIES: Dragon's egg, reddish-brown broom

YEAR
4
Harry Potter and the Goblet of Fire

Hungarian Horntail
⋙ FIRE~BREATHING DRAGON ⋙

Did you know?
The horns on the Hungarian Horntail are taken from the tail sections of LEGO dinosaur models. The tail includes two LEGO dinosaur neck pieces and a specially made end piece.

To create the most ferocious breed of dragon, LEGO designers used pieces from other terrible lizards. They also picked out scary details on the fire-breathing head, such as the eyes and teeth, in gold paint, and used two hinges on each of the large wings.

The dragon's head is hinged so that the mouth opens and closes.

The wing claws are tan coloured LEGO banana pieces.

The wings flap up and down on strong hinges.

Transparent, bright orange flame pieces are used in other sets as water (coloured blue) and seaweed (coloured green).

DATA FILE
SETS: 4767 Harry and the Hungarian Horntail (2005)
PIECES: 27
ACCESSORIES: None

The legs and body come as a single immovable piece.

Professor Dumbledore
BEARDED WIZARD

For his later minifigures, LEGO designers have dressed Professor Dumbledore in different coloured robes and have removed his cloak (p.21). With the 2010 minifigure, he has a reversible head – one side appears stern, while the other side is smiling and has no glasses.

Behind the beard
Dumbledore's 2010 minifigure features an updated sand blue outfit. Beneath his beard, he wears a jacket and a light brown embroidered shirt that is fastened by four silver buttons.

The 2010 minifigure has new eyebrows and gold-rimmed glasses, while the 2005 variant has black glasses (below).

All four Dumbledore minifigures use the same shaped piece for his beard.

The torso has swirling silver and purple decorations.

VARIANTS

SETS: 4767 Harry and the Hungarian Horntail (2005), 5378 Hogwarts Castle (2007)
PIECES: 5
ACCESSORIES: Potion bottle

DATA FILE

SETS: 4842 Hogwarts Castle (2010), 852982 Magnet set
PIECES: 5
ACCESSORIES: Tan wand

Mad-Eye Moody
ONE-LEGGED WIZARD

Moody's hair piece is mostly used on female LEGO minifigures, but is also found on male Harry Potter minifigures, such as Snape (p.26) and Lucius Malfoy (p.40).

With his magical eye that can see in any direction, Alastor "Mad-Eye" Moody is an intimidating figure. LEGO designers recreated his imposing manner and unique appearance with this 2005 minifigure.

DATA FILE

SETS: 4767 Harry and the Hungarian Horntail (2005)
PIECES: 4
ACCESSORIES: None

The unique face features scars and a magical false eye.

The torso is painted with a buckled jacket and a light grey shirt.

Moody's minifigure has a pirate peg-leg instead of the standard LEGO hip and legs pieces.

Moody's minifigure is unique to Harry and the Hungarian Horntail (set 4767), where he is overseeing the Triwizard Tournament.

Did you know?
In the movies, Mad-Eye Moody's left leg is his peg-leg, but for his LEGO minifigure, his right leg is the peg-leg, as this is standard for all LEGO peg-leg minifigures.

Harry Potter and the Goblet of Fire

YEAR
4

87

Harry Potter
SECOND TASK SWIMMER

For the second test of the Triwizard Tournament (p.84), the four champions have to face the underwater merpeople in set 4762. Harry's minifigure is dressed for this aquatic adventure in a swimming outfit and has a reversible head to show the effects of Gillyweed, a magical plant, which when eaten, gives a person gills and webbing between the fingers and toes.

The reversible head piece has gills printed on one side.

Harry carries a shiny chrome knife.

Did you know?
LEGO designers used a chef's hat to create a jellyfish in Rescue from the Merpeople (set 4762).

This minifigure was the first in the Harry Potter theme to feature flesh-coloured legs and a different colour hip piece to represent swimming trunks.

The torso is printed with the swimming outfit of the Hogwarts champion.

The orange flipper pieces attach to the bottom of each foot.

DATA FILE

SETS: 4762 Rescue from the Merpeople (2005)
PIECES: 6
ACCESSORIES: Chrome knife

Viktor Krum

SECOND TASK SHARK

The shark's head is moulded with eyes and razor-sharp teeth in its jaws.

The Durmstrang champion has a unique approach to the underwater challenge – he partially Transfigures into a shark! LEGO designers achieved this transformation by developing a shark's head that fits over Krum's head piece.

DATA FILE

SETS: 4762 Rescue from the Merpeople (2005)
PIECES: 4
ACCESSORIES: Shark head

Krum's torso is printed with the Durmstrang crest, which is a double-headed eagle.

Like Harry, Krum's swimming costume has different coloured legs and hip pieces.

Human head
Beneath the shark's head is Krum's human face. It features a hint of chin whiskers and also comes with a flat-cut hair piece.

Did you know?
The Rescue from the Merpeople (set 4762) features a small underwater cave which, when pushed from behind, shoots a small lobster out across the room.

Ron Weasley
UNDERWATER CAPTIVE

As part of his second task in the Triwizard Tournament, Harry has to rescue his best friend from the underwater merpeople. Both Ron and Hermione's heads show the students under the spell of the inhabitants of the black lake.

This side of the reversible head shows Ron enchanted.

Wide awake
The other side of Ron's reversible head shows him wide awake and with a grin that leans a little to his right (while his variant's face, below, leans the other way). No doubt he is more than a little relieved at being rescued by Harry!

DATA FILE

SETS: 4762 Rescue from the Merpeople (2005), 5378 Hogwarts Castle (2007)
PIECES: 4
ACCESSORIES: None

The 2005 minifigures have the same uniform as the variants released in 2004.

Did you know?
Set 4762 features a lever to jettison Hermione and Ron to safety, away from the merpeople.

VARIANTS

SETS: 4757 Hogwarts Castle (2004)
PIECES: 4
ACCESSORIES: None

Hermione Granger

AQUATIC HOSTAGE

VARIANTS

SETS: 5378
Hogwarts Castle
(2007)
PIECES: 4
ACCESSORIES:
Magnifying glass

SETS: 4738 Hagrid's
Hut (2010), 4842
Hogwarts Castle
(2010), 852982
Magnet set
PIECES: 4
ACCESSORIES:
Reddish-brown
wand

Hermione has an unexpected role during the second task of the Triwizard Tournament. Both she and Ron are chosen to be held captive by the merpeople. Her LEGO minifigure shows she is enchanted during this escapade so that she can survive underwater.

With her eyes closed, Hermione is under the spell of the merpeople.

The variant released in 2007 (above left), is almost identical to this one, except for a different hair piece and without the enchanted face.

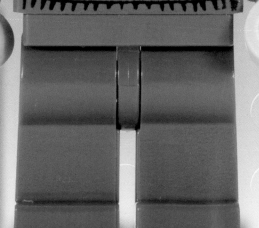

Knowing smile

The other side of Hermione's reversible head shows her awake once the merpeople's enchantment has been lifted. Perhaps her smile is because she has been rescued by Viktor Krum (p.89).

DATA FILE

SETS: 4762 Rescue from the Merpeople (2005)
PIECES: 4
ACCESSORIES: None

THE LEGO designers created this exclusive minifigure to accompany the publication of the trade edition of Dorling Kindersley's *LEGO Harry Potter Building the Magical World*. The minifigure shows Harry ready to attend the Yule Ball, an event held during each Triwizard Tournament.

Harry's hair piece is found on a further 31 LEGO minifigures, including a young Anakin Skywalker from the LEGO® *Star Wars*™ theme.

Harry's exclusive minifigure comes with a reversible head with one side smiling and the other frowning.

Dressed for the ball, Harry wears a black waistcoat fastened with silver buttons, and a white shirt and bow tie.

The black waistcoat reveals the white sleeves of the shirt that Harry is wearing.

DATA FILE
→◆←

SETS: N/A
PIECES: 4
ACCESSORIES: None

YEAR 4   Harry Potter and the Goblet of Fire

Merperson
UNDERWATER GUARDIAN

Deep beneath the surface of the black lake lurk mysterious beings known as merpeople. LEGO designers included one in set 4762 to guard Ron and Hermione. His stern face and terrifying weapon show that this merperson means business!

The merpeople defend the black lake using these fearsome LEGO pikes.

The merperson minifigure comes with an unposeable single-piece fish tail with a unique printed pattern.

The merperson has green skin, with scales printed on his fishy surface.

Under the sea
Trapped beneath a submerged arch, Ron and Hermione wait to be rescued by Harry and Krum (pp.90–91) while surrounded by a host of other aquatic creatures.

DATA FILE

SETS: 4762 Rescue from the Merpeople (2005)
PIECES: 4
ACCESSORIES: Medium blue pike

Skeletons
WALKING DEAD

Whether it is the creepy surroundings of Diagon Alley (set 10217) or the eerie setting for the Graveyard Duel (set 4766), no spooky LEGO set is complete without a skeleton minifigure. LEGO designers have created four variants to go with the Harry Potter theme.

The torso piece comes with exposed ribs and backbone.

The skeleton's skull is made from a white version of a standard LEGO head piece.

This variant's head is printed with a happy-looking face.

The poseable legs allow the skeleton to walk. Spooky!

All the skeleton variants use the same shaped head, torso and leg pieces.

Did you know?
In Diagon Alley (set 10217), the skeleton lives in the shop window of Borgin and Burkes.

YEAR 4   Harry Potter and the Goblet of Fire

The scarier version of the face has slanted eyes, narrower nostrils and a wicked grin.

Winged skeleton

The grave of Tom Riddle stands in the creepy graveyard at Little Hangleton. Perched over the LEGO headstone is a skeleton figure complete with large, outspread wings and a sinister black hood.

DATA FILE

SETS: 4766 Graveyard Duel (2005)
PIECES: 6
ACCESSORIES: None

The scary skull was originally designed for the LEGO Alpha Team Mission Deep Sea range.

The black and green skeleton variants are unique to the LEGO Harry Potter theme.

This green skeleton has the same torso piece as the Dementors (p.66).

DATA FILE

SETS: 4766 Graveyard Duel (2005)
PIECES: 6
ACCESSORIES: None

Did you know?

The first skeleton minifigures had ball-and-socket joints, which allowed the arms to move in all directions. These were later replaced with more restricted shoulder joints.

Harry Potter
DUELLING WIZARD

When he completes the final task of the Triwizard Tournament, Harry is transported to a sinister graveyard where he must face his nemesis – Lord Voldemort. As part of the Graveyard Duel (set 4766), LEGO designers have kept Harry in his Triwizard's uniform.

Cracking crypts
Set 4766 comes with everything you would expect to find in a graveyard – a shovel, a cart, coffins, headstones, black owls and a host of spooky skeletons (pp.94–95).

Harry wears the black and red Tournament shirt to take part in the final Triwizard task – navigating the maze to find the Triwizard Cup.

Harry's Tournament uniform is divided in half, with different-coloured sleeves.

Did you know?
Set 4766 recreates the graveyard where Lord Voldemort's father, Tom Riddle Senior, is buried.

DATA FILE
SETS: 4766 Graveyard Duel (2005)
PIECES: 4
ACCESSORIES: Black wand

YEAR 4   Harry Potter and the Goblet of Fire

Death Eater
MALEVOLENT MALFOY

DATA FILE

SETS: 4766 Graveyard
Duel (2005)
PIECES: 5
ACCESSORIES: Cloak

The arrival of the Dark Lord is witnessed by his followers, the Death Eaters. Chief among these is Lucius Malfoy and to accompany the Graveyard Duel (set 4766), LEGO designers gave this minifigure a reversible head, one side of which has the sinister Death Eater mask.

Malfoy's face has raised eyebrows and a slight frown.

Updated mask
The other side of Malfoy's reversible head features a black Death Eater mask. This version has sinister eye holes and a terrifying skull-like grin.

This cloak is also found on the minifigures of Lord Voldemort (p.99) and the Dementors (p.66).

Under the cloth cloak, Malfoy wears a pinstripe jacket, a blue tie and a waistcoat.

Peter Pettigrew
SERVANT OF THE DARK LORD

Although he was a close companion to Harry's mother and father, Peter Pettigrew was secretly in the service of the Dark Lord. The LEGO Group has recreated the devious traitor in two sets with two variants, one of which comes with his Animagus form: Ron's pet rat Scabbers (p.69).

(p.69)

VARIANTS

SETS: 4756 Shrieking Shack (2004)
PIECES: 3
ACCESSORIES: None

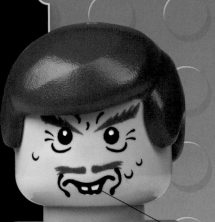

The later variant has a magical grey right hand – a gift from Voldemort to replace the one that he cut off in order to bring the Dark Lord back to life.

Pettigrew's face is printed with two protruding teeth – a reminder of his Animagus form.

DATA FILE

SETS: 4766 Graveyard Duel (2005)
PIECES: 4
ACCESSORIES: Chrome silver knife

Standing rat
The Shrieking Shack (set 4756) comes with a small standing model of Ron's pet rat, Scabbers – a hint at the creature's hidden human form.

Lord Voldemort

HE WHO MUST NOT BE NAMED

DATA FILE

SETS: 4766 Graveyard Duel (2005)
PIECES: 4
ACCESSORIES: Black wand, cloak

Having appeared on one side of Professor Quirrell's head (p.27), Lord Voldemort makes his first full LEGO minifigure appearance in The Graveyard Duel (set 4766). The set recreates the moment when Peter Pettigrew helps the Dark Lord to return to his full human form.

On this minifigure variant, Voldemort's head glows in the dark.

Beneath the Death Eater's cloak (p.97), Voldemort has a plain black torso and legs, with white hands.

Did you know?

This version of Voldemort features a face similar to the one used on the back of Quirrell's head, only the nostrils are smaller and the red eyes are now clear.

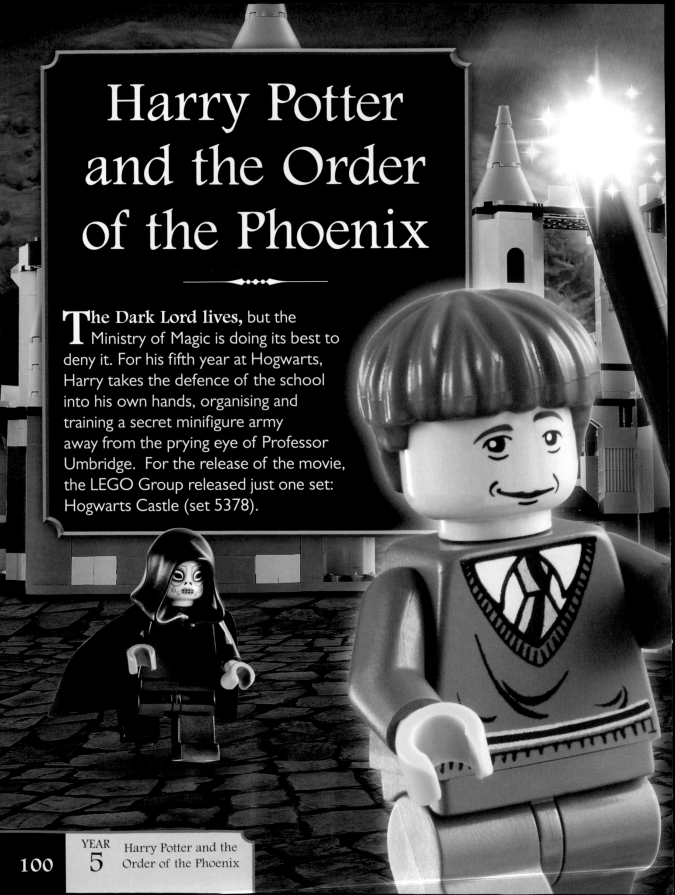

Harry Potter and the Order of the Phoenix

The Dark Lord lives, but the Ministry of Magic is doing its best to deny it. For his fifth year at Hogwarts, Harry takes the defence of the school into his own hands, organising and training a secret minifigure army away from the prying eye of Professor Umbridge. For the release of the movie, the LEGO Group released just one set: Hogwarts Castle (set 5378).

5378 Hogwarts Castle (2007)

Harry Potter and the
Order of the Phoenix
YEAR
5
101

Luna Lovegood
⊷⊷ RAVENCLAW STUDENT ⊷⊷

On board the Hogwarts Express (set 4841), Harry, Ginny and Ron are joined by Luna Lovegood. This quirky minifigure is a member of Ravenclaw house and is unique to this set.

Seeing things
The other side of Luna's reversible head features a large pair of Spectrespecs. According to Luna, these glasses let wizards see Wrackspurts and come with an ornate gold frame and red- and blue-coloured lenses for each eye.

The front of Luna's reversible head features her smiling face and her wonky eyebrows.

Printed on top of Luna's trousers is a brightly coloured skirt, with circles, stars, hearts, horses and birds, to reflect Luna's unique style.

The front of Luna's unique torso features a bright pink jacket.

The minifigure comes with a copy of *The Quibbler*, which is edited by Luna's father, Xenophilius.

Did you know?
Luna Lovegood is the only member of Ravenclaw house to be shown as a student in a LEGO® set.

DATA FILE

SETS: 4841 Hogwarts Express (2010)
PIECES: 4
ACCESSORIES: *The Quibbler* magazine tile

YEAR **5** Harry Potter and the Order of the Phoenix

Thestral
→ SKELETAL STEEDS →

The Thestral's leathery wings are recreated using thick, ridged plastic pieces.

The wings can flap up and down, but the body is unposeable.

These skeletal creatures are not visible to everyone and have been uniquely created from black LEGO elements for Hogwarts Castle (set 5378). The Thestrals can carry minifigures as they fly through the air and pull carriages.

DATA FILE
→◆◆◆←

SETS: 5378 Hogwarts Castle (2007)
PIECES: 5
ACCESSORIES: None

The wings are fixed to the body using special clip tiles.

The middle of the Thestral's body has a space for a minifigure to stand.

Did you know?
The Thestrals use the same skeleton body from other LEGO sets, except these are black and have wings.

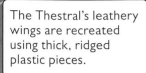

Draco Malfoy
◂•►— SLYTHERIN SPY —◂•►

Pacing the corridors of Hogwarts Castle (set 5378), Draco Malfoy will stop at nothing to defeat Harry and the other members of Dumbledore's Army. The minifigure's face was updated in 2007, and again in 2010, and he was given a slicked-back hairstyle to match his appearance in the movies.

Draco's updated head is still printed with a sneer and the hair piece is slightly more textured than on previous minifigures.

Draco's Slytherin tie features the silhouette of the house symbol – a coiled snake.

This version of the Slytherin uniform has the snake crest that is not featured on the 2007 variant (above).

Did you know?
Hogwarts Castle (set 5378) was the only LEGO set released exclusively for the movie *Harry Potter and the Order of the Phoenix*.

DATA FILE
◂••►

SETS: 4841 Hogwarts
Express (2010), 852983
Magnet Set (2010)
PIECES: 4
ACCESSORIES:
Black wand

104

YEAR
5   Harry Potter and the
Order of the Phoenix

Professor Snape
SCOWLING PROFESSOR

For the 2007 and 2010 minifigures of Professor Snape, LEGO designers updated the Head of Slytherin's face, giving him a deeper scowl and thicker frown lines. The later variant also has a new hair piece.

The new hair piece features a tousled style with a centre parting.

From 2007, flesh-coloured heads replaced the glow-in-the-dark heads used on earlier Snape minifigures.

Details of Professor Snape's robe and waistcoat, including the buttons, are picked out in silver.

The all-black outfit replaces the purple frock coats worn on the 2001 and 2004 variants (p.26).

DATA FILE

SETS: 4842 Hogwarts Castle (2010), 852983 Magnet Set
PIECES: 5
ACCESSORIES: Cloak, black wand

Professor McGonagall
DEPUTY HEADMISTRESS

The Deputy Headmistress of Hogwarts is recreated with a stern looking minifigure in Dumbledore's Office (set 4729). However, for Hogwarts Castle (set 4842), LEGO designers have given her a slight smile, while keeping her ornate robes and hat.

DATA FILE

SETS: 4842 Hogwarts Castle (2010)
PIECES: 5
ACCESSORIES: Cloak

The 2010 variant's face has different dimples and age lines from the earlier model (below).

McGonagall is the only LEGO Harry Potter minifigure to wear a green wizard's hat.

Both variants of Professor McGonagall wear robes that are fastened at the neck by a large, hoop-shaped clasp.

VARIANTS

SETS: 4729 Dumbledore's Office (2002)
PIECES: 5
ACCESSORIES: Cloak, chrome brass key

Professor McGonagall's 2010 minifigure comes with a darker green cloak than the 2002 variant (left).

Professor Umbridge
PINK PROFESSOR

Professor Umbridge's face is painted with streaks of thick pink make-up and a sour expression.

Professor **Umbridge** looks sweet, but acts tough. Her minifigure comes with decorative kitten plates and cute pink accessories, but her scowl shows that she will tolerate no mischief from Harry and his disobedient friends.

Kitten plates
Professor Umbridge's office in Hogwarts Castle (set 5378) is decorated with a pink quill holder, bright pink flowers and LEGO bricks printed with kitten plates.

Did you know?
Professor Umbridge's thick curly hair piece is only found in one other set: Green Grocer (set 10185) from the LEGO Modular Buildings theme.

A kitten brooch is printed onto the minifigure's torso.

The scarf and pocket details are picked out in a darker pink.

To complete her outfit, Professor Umbridge's leg and hip pieces match the bright pink torso and make-up. These pink legs are unique to this minifigure.

DATA FILE
SETS: 5378 Hogwarts Castle (2007)
PIECES: 4
ACCESSORIES: Kitten plates bricks, Harry's confiscated broom, pink flowers, pink cup

Creatures

Many of the LEGO® Harry Potter™ sets come with their own miniature zoo of amazing animals. Some of these creatures crop up in surprising places, shapes and colours, adding to the unexpected nature of the Harry Potter theme. These include a fish that's nowhere near its home, spider pieces in an array of amazing shades and a lobster created from a familiar LEGO piece.

Detailed bat
This dark bluish-grey variant clearly shows the details in the bat's wings and feet.

Black bat
The black bat appears in 11 Harry Potter sets, including four versions of Hogwarts.

Slippery customer
This pearlescent light grey fish piece is part of two LEGO Harry Potter sets – and neither of them are near the sea! They are Diagon Alley (set 10217) and Hagrid's Hut (set 4738).

Cats
This crouching unmarked white cat is only found among the magical shops of Diagon Alley (set 4723).

Scorpions
Scorpions come in two colours in the Harry Potter theme. These are dark grey and transparent neon orange.

Weasleys' pig
With a sty that backs onto the kitchen, this pig is very much a part of the Weasley family home, The Burrow (set 4840). The flesh-coloured pig has black eyes with white highlights added.

Crab
This aquatic animal appears in Rescue from the Merpeople (set 4762).

Jellyfish
Floating through set 4762, this transparent blue jellyfish is also found in white on the heads of 19 LEGO chef minifigures.

Lobster
It might look like a scorpion, but this red piece is actually a lobster and shoots out of an underwater cave in set 4762.

Octopus
The ends of this octopus's arms can wrap around the studs of LEGO bricks, holding the octopus in place in set 4762.

Neon orange
This brightly coloured arachnid is partially transparent, giving it an eerie appearance.

Neon green
Crawling around Snape's Class (set 4705), this spider is found in five more Harry Potter sets.

Common spider
The black variant is found in 43 LEGO sets, including 11 from the Harry Potter theme.

Transparent red spider
With a hole on the underside of its body, this transparent red spider can fix itself to any part of Hogwarts Castle (set 4757).

Orange spider
This orange arachnid is easy to spot as it scuttles around four LEGO Harry Potter sets.

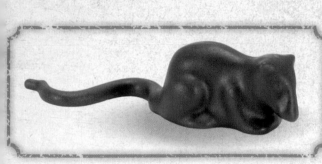

Reddish-brown rat
Part of two Harry Potter sets, this variant is scuttling around Hagrid's Hut (set 4754) and Sirius Black's Escape (set 4753).

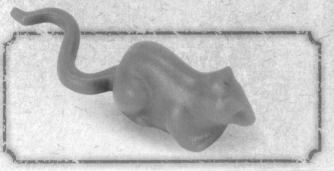

Dark grey rat
The dark grey variant is only found in one Harry Potter set: Diagon Alley Shops (set 4723).

Light grey rat
Found in four LEGO Harry Potter sets in total, the light grey rodent variant may represent Ron's pet rat, Scabbers.

White rat
This rat is part of Gringotts Bank (set 4714), Hagrid's Hut (set 4707) and Hogwarts Castle (set 4709).

Professor Flitwick
◆►• CHARMS EXPERT •◄◆

Professor Flitwick, the Charms teacher at Hogwarts, is also the Head of Ravenclaw house and one of the shortest professors at Hogwarts. To capture the character of this quirky professor, the minifigure has the same hairstyle as the early Ron minifigures (p.69) and is dressed for dinner in the Great Hall.

Large, bushy eyebrows sit above Flitwick's glasses.

The unique head is printed with silver-rimmed glasses and a bushy moustache.

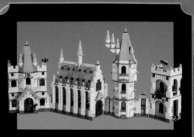

Hogwarts Castle
For the fourth version of Hogwarts Castle (set 4842), LEGO designers included the Main Hall and three other sections: the Astronomy Tower, the Gryffindor and Slytherin common rooms and Dumbeldore's Office.

The smartly dressed professor's torso is printed with a waistcoat and large bow tie, which is also worn by Griphook the goblin (p.13).

DATA FILE
◆━◆◆◆━◆

SETS: 4842 Hogwarts Castle (2010)
PIECES: 4
ACCESSORIES: Reddish-brown wand

Professor Flitwick has short, unposeable legs to reflect his small stature.

Did you know?
Actor Warwick Davis has three minifigures of characters he has portrayed – Flitwick, Griphook and Wicket from LEGO® Star Wars™.

Argus Filch

GROUCHY CARETAKER

Mrs Norris
Prowling the corridors of Hogwarts Castle (set 4842) is Filch's cat, Mrs Norris. Her face is printed with a pink nose, white cheeks, whiskers and three dark stripes on her forehead.

This bad-tempered minifigure is only found in the halls and corridors of Hogwarts Castle (set 4842). He tours the school with a large bunch of keys jangling from a chain on his waist. This minifigure has made it his mission to spoil Harry's plans, even going so far as to help Professor Umbridge (p.107).

Filch's grumpy face is printed with frown lines, stern eyes, a down-turned mouth and grey stubble.

His unique torso shows Filch wearing a dark-grey jacket with a crumpled vest, creased shirt and an undone tie.

Filch's legs are printed with a belt and a set of keys hanging from them.

DATA FILE

SETS: 4842 Hogwarts Castle (2010)
PIECES: 4
ACCESSORIES: Torch, key

Did you know?
Filch's prototype minifigure had brown hair and used Boba Fett's head from LEGO *Star Wars*. Those were replaced with grey hair and Filch's real head when the minifigure was released.

Harry Potter

·❖· ARMY LEADER ·❖·

Dark times during Harry's fifth year at Hogwarts Castle (set 5378) force him to create Dumbledore's Army to stand against Lord Voldemort. LEGO designers revised his face, giving him a slight smile and raising his eyebrows above his glasses.

DATA FILE
·◆·◆·

SETS: 5378 Hogwarts Castle (2007)
PIECES: 4
ACCESSORIES: Black wand

Harry's uniform features the scarlet and gold stripes of Gryffindor, but without the house crest.

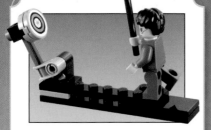

Spell target
Dumbledore's Army meets in the Room of Requirement to train. The LEGO Group has recreated one important piece of training equipment – a spell target. The target topples over if it is hit by a well-aimed spell.

This Harry minifigure from 2007 features the boy wizard wearing grey trousers for the last time.

Although this minifigure is only found in the 2007 Hogwarts Castle (set 5378), it uses the same torso as the cloaked 2004 minifigure (p.74).

Death Eater
SPELL TARGET

Only released with the 2007 version of Hogwarts Castle (set 5378), this sinister, faceless Death Eater is actually harmless. It is a dummy that stands inside the Room of Requirement, where Harry and Dumbledore's Army use it as a target to practise their spells upon.

Hogwarts
The third version of Hogwarts Castle (set 5378) released in 2007 features three separate buildings. These are the main castle, the Room of Requirement and the greenhouse.

While other Death Eater masks appear on the other side of Lucius Malfoy's head (p.132), this minifigure is anonymous and has no other face.

A Death Eater's mask has snake-like eye slits.

The Death Eater's torso and legs are black and featureless.

DATA FILE
SETS: 5378 Hogwarts Castle (2007)
PIECES: 5
ACCESSORIES: Cloak

Ron Weasley

For this minifigure of Ron, released in 2010 with Hagrid's Hut (set 4738), LEGO designers revised his Gryffindor uniform. His new outfit features the coloured stripes and the gold and scarlet crest of Gryffindor house.

This hair piece is the same as on Ron's other 2010 variant (p.127).

Did you know?
The model for Hagrid's Hut (set 4738) features a fireplace that lights up with a warming glow. This was the first time such an effect had been used in a LEGO Harry Potter set.

The reversible head features a scared face on the other side.

This minifigure of Ron is unique to Hagrid's Hut (set 4738).

Half-giant's hut
There have been three models of Hagrid's Hut. The 2010 version (set 4738) opens out to reveal shelves packed with potion bottles, a cauldron over the fire and Norbert, Hagrid's pet baby dragon. As well as Hagrid, the set comes with uniformed minifigures of Ron, Harry and Hermione.

DATA FILE
SETS: 4738 Hagrid's Hut (2010)
PIECES: 4
ACCESSORIES: Reddish-brown wand

Harry Potter
⋙ INVISIBLE WIZARD ⋘

This Cloak is only found in two LEGO Harry Potter sets (4841 and 4842).

Under the rule of Professor Umbridge (p.107), Hogwarts is a difficult place to sneak about. Fortunately, Harry has a magical cloak that makes him invisible. Now he can sneak past Filch and Umbridge's spies undetected.

The Cloak used to cover the minifigures is made from iridescent material.

Beneath the Cloak
Hiding under the Cloak in set 4842 is this minifigure. It can also be found in a further five sets: Freeing Dobby (set 4736), Hagrid's Hut (set 4738), Hogwarts (set 4867), The Forbidden Forest (set 4865) and The Lab (set 30111).

DATA FILE
◆◆◆◆
SETS: 4841 Hogwarts Express (2010), 4842 Hogwarts Castle (2010)
PIECES: 4
ACCESSORIES: Reddish-brown wand, Invisibility Cloak

Harry Potter and the Half-Blood Prince

The **LEGO Group** only released one set in 2010 relating to *Harry Potter and the Half-Blood Prince*. The Burrow (set 4840) recreates the scene when a vicious group of Death Eater minifigures attacks the Weasleys' home. This set includes several minifigures making their first appearance in the LEGO® Harry Potter™ theme, including Bellatrix Lestrange, Fenrir Greyback and Arthur and Molly Weasley. Other sets released in this year recreate events from earlier movies.

4840 The Burrow (2010)

Harry Potter
✦ BATTLING WIZARD ✦

When the Death Eaters attack The Burrow (set 4840), Harry is there to help his friends the Weasleys fight them off. This minifigure features a reversible head – one side has a smile for his friends, the other side has a determined expression for facing the Death Eaters.

Floo Network
The mechanical fireplace in The Burrow (set 4840) is actually an opening to the magical Floo Network. Flicking the switch on the side flips the hearth back, revealing a flash of green flames. When the switch is flicked back, the orange flames return and the minifigure has gone!

DATA FILE
✦•◦•✦

SETS: 4840 The Burrow (2010), 4866 The Knight Bus (2011), 10217 Diagon Alley (2011)
PIECES: 4
ACCESSORIES: Reddish-brown wand

Harry wears an open jacket and a light blue t-shirt – an outfit similar to that of his 2001 minifigure (p.10), but with black legs instead of tan.

This minifigure has black hips and legs, while the variant has dark bluish-grey legs.

VARIANTS
✦•◦•✦

SETS: 4841 Hogwarts Express (2010), 30110 Trolley (2011)
PIECES: 4
ACCESSORIES: Reddish-brown wand

YEAR 6 Harry Potter and the Half-Blood Prince

Ginny Weasley
━━◆ READY FOR BATTLE ◆━━

For her most recent minifigure version, Ginny boasts an updated hairstyle and face from previous models. While her other 2010 version shows her in her Hogwarts uniform, LEGO designers dressed her in casual clothes for the battle at The Burrow (set 4840).

Knitting pattern
LEGO designers have continued the pattern of Ginny's cardigan onto the reverse side of the minifigure's torso.

The two sides of the reversible head feature frowning and smiling faces.

Ginny now has a longer hair piece than her earliest version (p.43). This is unique to her 2010 versions.

Ginny's torso is printed with the design of a knitted zipped-up cardigan.

The unique trouser legs feature belt loops and pockets.

Did you know?
The Burrow (set 4840) features special bricks printed with editions of the *Daily Prophet* and *The Quibbler.*

DATA FILE

SETS: 4840 The Burrow (2010)
PIECES: 4
ACCESSORIES: Tan wand

Molly Weasley
WIZARD MOTHER

The Burrow (set 4840), includes three members of the Weasley clan. The family matriarch, Molly, is shown ready for anything the house can throw at her. As with all Weasley family members, she has a mop of bright orange hair.

Secured tightly
LEGO designers have carried the details of Molly's outfit onto the back of her torso. It is printed with the pattern of her cardigan and the tied strings of her apron.

DATA FILE
SETS: 4840 The Burrow (2010)
PIECES: 4
ACCESSORIES: None

Molly's torso is printed with a tan-coloured cardigan, neck scarf and the upper half of an orange apron.

Molly keeps balls of wool and needles in her apron pocket in case any knitting is needed at short notice.

The apron is decorated with swirls and flowers.

Molly's trousers are covered with the lower half of her apron.

Did you know?
Molly's hair piece is the same shape as the hair piece used on the first Hermione minifigure (p.16), but coloured dark orange instead of brown.

Arthur Weasley

◄► MINISTRY EMPLOYEE ◄►

The head of the Weasley household bears a strong resemblance to all of his sons. This is thanks to LEGO designers using the same hair piece as Fred and George (p.128), and a broad, lop-sided grin that is similar to all three Weasley boy minifigures.

Twisted building
The Burrow (set 4840) is a three-storey building whose unique twisted shape contains a kitchen and two bedrooms. Also in the set is a patch of marsh that hides a deadly secret (p.125).

Arthur's face is printed with cheek dimples and lines under the mouth and eyes.

Arthur wears a sand green jacket over his open-necked shirt and matching jumper.

The jacket details include four front pockets printed in black outline.

Mr Weasley works for the Ministry of Magic, but his minifigure is casually dressed for a day at the Burrow, with light bluish-grey trousers and a checked shirt.

DATA FILE

SETS: 4840 The Burrow (2010)
PIECES: 4
ACCESSORIES: Light bluish-grey wand, *The Quibbler* magazine tile

Double-sided heads

Since the introduction of the Professor Quirrell minifigure (p.27), double-sided heads have become a regular feature in the LEGO® universe, and the Harry Potter theme in particular. To increase the playability of the minifigures, LEGO designers have given them two very different expressions, a mask to hide their features or a completely different face altogether!

Bellatrix Lestrange

One side of Lestrange's head shows her cackling, evil side (top) as she attacks The Burrow (set 4840), while the other side shows her worried as Harry and his friends fight off the Death Eaters.

Draco Malfoy

This double-sided head of Draco's comes with Quidditch Match (set 4737) and Hogwarts Express (set 4841). One side (right) shows him with his usual arrogant sneer for when he's baiting Harry and his friends, while the other (left) shows him in a much more worried state, complete with trembling bottom lip.

Fenrir Greyback

As a werewolf, Greyback does not have a wide range of emotions – he's either snarling in anger (left) or he's scowling fiercely (right). Whether he's prowling around the shops of Diagon Alley (set 10217) or firing flaming torches at The Burrow (set 4840), Greyback has a villainous expression.

Ginny Weasley

Like Hermione, one side of Ginny's head shows a kind, smiling face (top), while the other side shows her with the determined look of a witch who is not to be crossed.

Harry Potter

Used on Harry's minifigures from 2010 onwards, this version of his double-sided head appears on six different variants. One side shows his kind, friendly smile, while the other features a stern, determined expression.

Mr Ollivander

As part of Diagon Alley (set 10217), Mr Ollivander is kidnapped by Fenrir Greyback and the Death Eaters during *Harry Potter and the Deathly Hallows*. The other side of his reversible head (right) shows his terror at these events.

Hermione Granger

As well as smiling (top), Hermione's other expression shows her with a determined scowl on her face. This can be used when confronting the Death Eaters – or when she is annoyed with Harry or Ron!

Ron Weasley

Of all of Harry's friends, Ron is the only one who does not feature a determined look on the other side of his reversible head. Instead, his mouth is twisted down and his teeth are clenched tightly together in an expression of pure panic!

Bellatrix Lestrange
FEMALE DEATH EATER

To portray the evil nature of Bellatrix Lestrange, her LEGO minifigure features a hideous, cackling mouth and eyes surrounded by dark make-up. She is dressed in a sumptuous gown to match the long, flowing locks of her thick black hair piece.

DATA FILE

SETS: 4840 The Burrow (2010)
PIECES: 4
ACCESSORIES: Black wand, flaming torches

Bellatrix's reversible head shows her laughing with fiendish glee on one side and looking terrified at defeat on the other.

This long hair piece is unique to her minifigure.

The torso and leg pieces are painted with an ornate silver and blue outfit.

The patterned skirt piece is made from a single sloping brick, so it is unposeable.

Did you know?
The Burrow (set 4840) contains three minifigures that are not seen anywhere else in the LEGO Harry Potter theme. These are Bellatrix Lestrange, and Arthur and Molly Weasley.

Flaming torches
To replicate the flaming torches used by the Death Eaters to attack The Burrow (set 4840), LEGO designers have used transparent yellow cones with orange flaming pieces attached to one end.

Fenrir Greyback
⟶ SAVAGE WEREWOLF ⟶

The werewolf Fenrir Greyback is a vicious member of Lord Voldemort's followers. Unlike Professor Lupin's model (p.67), Greyback's minifigure is always a werewolf, so he does not come with a werewolf's head. Instead, his body and face are permanently covered in hair and his silvery eyes have no pupils.

The marshes
LEGO designers recreated the marshland around The Burrow (set 4840) using long reed pieces. These are tall enough to hide a Death Eater minifigure and a catapult to launch flaming torches at the Weasley home.

Greyback's reversible head shows him baring his terrifying teeth on one side, while the other side shows him with a brooding, evil scowl.

Greyback's shirt is open to reveal his hairy wolf chest.

The unique torso is printed with a black jacket, grey shirt and an orange belt.

DATA FILE

SETS: 4840 The Burrow (2010), 10217 Diagon Alley (2011)
PIECES: 4
ACCESSORIES: Black wand, catapult

Hermione Granger
MUGGLE-BORN WITCH

This minifigure of Hermione is dressed in casual clothing, ready for a trip around the magical shops of Diagon Alley (set 10217). As with most of the later Harry Potter theme minifigures, she has a reversible head, with one side smiling and the other frowning.

Hair style
Hermione's brown hair piece has braids that go around the sides and are tied together at the back.

Did you know?
This torso is identical to the one used for Ginny Weasley (p.119) from The Burrow (set 4840).

Hermione's torso is printed with a zipped-up cardigan and white t-shirt.

There are only two version of Hermione that show her in casual clothing rather than her school uniform.

Hermione's trousers are similar to those of Ginny Weasley (p.119), but without the belt loop and pocket details.

DATA FILE

SETS: 10217 Diagon Alley (2011)
PIECES: 4
ACCESSORIES: Reddish-brown wand

Ron Weasley
◦► HUMOROUS WIZARD ◄◦

Scared face
The other side of Ron's reversible head shows a very scared face. It features wide staring eyes and a broad mouth with teeth clenched firmly together.

This minifigure of Ron has an updated, older appearance for the teenage wizard. He also has the facial expression to suit the most frightening occasions, including coming across the Death Eaters in Diagon Alley (set 10217).

The bowl-shaped hairstyle from earlier variants (p.24) is now replaced with a tousled look that is unique to Ron's minifigure.

Ron's unique torso shows him wearing a tartan tank top.

Ron is one of 12 minifigures in Diagon Alley (set 10217) – more than any other LEGO Harry Potter set.

This minifigure has reddish-brown trousers to match his sleeves, while his 2010 variant wears black trousers (right).

VARIANTS

SETS: 4841 Hogwarts Express (2010)
PIECES: 4
ACCESSORIES: Reddish-brown wand

DATA FILE
◦►•◦◦•◄◦
SETS: 10217 Diagon Alley (2011)
PIECES: 4
ACCESSORIES: Reddish-brown wand

Fred and George
✦✦ TROUBLE~MAKING TWINS ✦✦

On leaving Hogwarts, the Weasley twins, Fred and George, establish their joke shop, Weasleys' Wizard Wheezes. As part of Diagon Alley (set 10217), the twins appear as a single minifigure, with a double-sided face – each side of the face represents a different twin.

George Weasley
The reverse side of the double-sided head shows George Weasley. His smile leans to his left and he is raising his left eyebrow ever so slightly.

Fred's smile is lop-sided to his right and shows more teeth than his brother. He is also raising his right eyebrow a little.

The twins are now smartly dressed to run their joke shop. They wear dark orange jackets, waistcoats, shirts and ties.

The legs and hip pieces are dark orange to match the torso.

Did you know?
Even though Weasleys' Wizard Wheezes is not part of Diagon Alley (set 10217), Fred and George can still be found roaming this detailed set.

DATA FILE
✦ ◆◆◆ ✦

SETS: 10217 Diagon Alley (2011)
PIECES: 4
ACCESSORIES: Marauder's Map

Harry Potter
EXCLUSIVE MINIFIGURE

Unique wizard
While this minifigure appears nowhere else apart from this book, it is not the only exclusive variant of Harry Potter. Another minifigure was created for Dorling Kindersley *LEGO Harry Potter Building the Magical World* (p.92).

Created exclusively for the trade edition of this book, this minifigure sees Harry dressed for a party. It is the 11th minifigure to show Harry out of any Hogwarts uniform, but the only one to see him wearing a smart collared shirt secured with a tie.

Harry wears a stylish red shirt and tie combination.

The torso and legs are printed with a long jacket and a vest fastened with silver buttons.

Harry's unique outfit is especially for the Slug Club Christmas Party – a gathering of select pupils chosen exclusively by Hogwarts teacher Professor Slughorn.

Did you know?
This is the 24th and final Harry Potter minifigure. He appears more than twice as many times as Hermione.

DATA FILE
SETS: N/A
PIECES: 4
ACCESSORIES: None

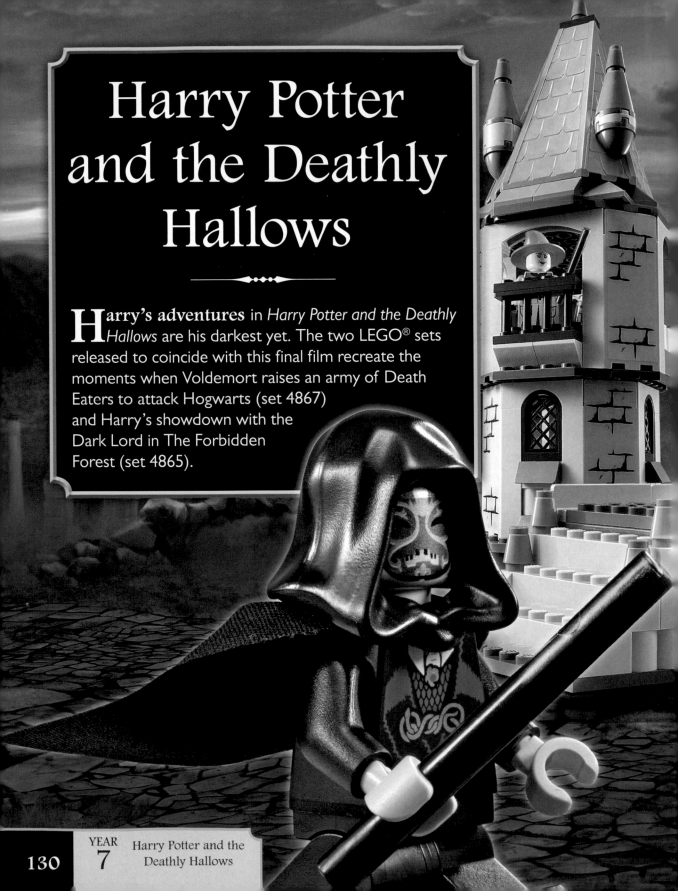

Harry Potter and the Deathly Hallows

Harry's adventures in *Harry Potter and the Deathly Hallows* are his darkest yet. The two LEGO® sets released to coincide with this final film recreate the moments when Voldemort raises an army of Death Eaters to attack Hogwarts (set 4867) and Harry's showdown with the Dark Lord in The Forbidden Forest (set 4865).

4867 Hogwarts (2011)

Lucius Malfoy
DEATH EATER

Most of the time, Lucius Malfoy appears to be a respectable citizen, visiting Diagon Alley (set 10217) or Hogwarts (set 4867). However, here he is shown to be a cruel character in the service of Lord Voldemort.

Death Eater mask
Turning around the reversible head on this minifigure will reveal the mask of a Death Eater. To complete the outfit, a dark hood can be added after removing the hair piece.

Lucius now has a thicker, longer blond hair piece.

This 2010 variant of Malfoy wears a dark green cravat around his neck.

Malfoy's pinstripe suit has been replaced with a purple-coloured smoking jacket.

DATA FILE

SETS: 4736 Freeing Dobby (2010), 10217 Diagon Alley (2011), 4867 Hogwarts (2011)
PIECES: 5
ACCESSORIES: Black wand, black hood, cloak

Mr Ollivander

WAND SHOP OWNER

DATA FILE

SETS: 10217 Diagon Alley (2011)
PIECES: 4
ACCESSORIES: Container with wands, wand boxes

Considered the finest supplier of magic wands, Mr Ollivander's wand shop takes pride of place in Diagon Alley (set 10217). The proprietor, Mr Ollivander, is a smartly dressed minifigure with grey hair and a face lined with age.

The head piece is topped with tousled grey hair and printed with grey stubble.

Ollivander's face looks shocked when he is kidnapped by the Death Eaters. The other side of the reversible head has a smile for his rescuers.

Ollivander's torso is printed with a brown jacket, buttoned waistcoat, ruffled shirt and a brown scarf.

Wand shop
Inside the jumbled wand shop are wand cases and bottles of potions. There is also a movable LEGO ladder so that Mr Ollivander can reach even the highest shelves.

Did you know?
The outside of the shop has a wanted poster showing the escaped prisoner Sirius Black (p.78).

Professor Sprout

◄•◄ HERBOLOGY TEACHER ►•►

Professor Sprout is the Head of Hufflepuff house. As the professor of Herbology she is usually found in the greenhouse tending to the Mandrake plants (p.50), but during the battle at Hogwarts (set 4867) she is found on the castle's towers fighting off the invading Death Eaters.

Professor Sprout's unique face is printed with a smiling mouth, grey eyebrows and age wrinkles.

Did you know?
The wizard hat worn by Professor Sprout is an updated version from earlier hats with a slight texture.

The professor wears a full-length dark tan coat covering her torso and unposeable leg piece.

The coat is fastened at the neck with a leaf-shaped clasp.

Sprout's overalls have printed pockets so that she can carry around any essential herbs.

DATA FILE

SETS: 4867 Hogwarts (2011)
PIECES: 4
ACCESSORIES:
Reddish-brown wand

Neville Longbottom
❖❖ HEROIC WIZARD ❖❖

This hair piece is found on other minifigures, including Marcus Flint and Oliver Wood (pp.46–47).

To capture the determination of this young wizard, LEGO designers have given Neville's minifigure a reversible head showing two very different expressions. While one side shows him smiling, the other shows the young wizard gritting his teeth, ready for battle.

Neville uses his wand to fight off the Death Eaters during the battle of Hogwarts.

Neville's mouth is printed with his distinctive protruding teeth, shown here gritted in determination.

Neville is shown wearing a button-up blue shirt and a grey patterned cardigan.

Hooded hero
The details printed on the back of Neville's torso continue the pattern from the front. They show that his knitted cardigan also has a hood to keep him warm on those cold winter nights at Hogwarts.

DATA FILE
❖❖❖❖❖

SETS: 4867 Hogwarts (2011)
PIECES: 4
ACCESSORIES: Reddish-brown wand

Accessories

It is often the little details that bring a LEGO® set to life. The magical world of LEGO® Harry Potter™ is bursting with colourful and unusual accessories that represent key objects from the films. All have been designed to be easily grasped by minifigures' hands. Some are common across other LEGO themes, while others have printing and detailing unique to the LEGO Harry Potter theme. Many more demonstrate the LEGO Group's ability to adapt standard pieces into new and exciting Harry Potter themed accessories.

Marauder's Map
Harry uses this Marauder's Map tile in Harry and the Marauder's Map (set 4751) to sneak around the castle.

Dobby's sock
To make a LEGO sock for Dobby's Release (set 4731), the LEGO Group printed this design on a versatile tile piece.

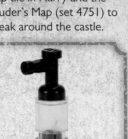

Lantern
Argus Filch's lantern in Hogwarts Castle (set 4842) is made by attaching a black tap and round plate to a yellow round piece.

Chocolate frog card
To create this hologram, a holographic image is printed on a sticker then transferred to a tile for sets 4708 and 4709.

Wizard's broom
This broom piece is a familiar sight across many LEGO sets and appears just as frequently throughout LEGO Harry Potter – for Quidditch matches and heroic adventures. It comes in black as well as various shades of brown.

Philosopher's Stone
Jewels appear in over 200 LEGO sets, but the red gem in The Final Challenge (set 4702) represents the Philosopher's Stone.

James Potter's Plaque
To celebrate Harry's father's achievements in Quidditch, this plaque appears in Hogwarts Castle (set 4842).

The Monster Book of Monsters
This LEGO book has descriptions of every magical beast.

Glass goblet
The goblet piece can be found in different shades of blue and green, for feasting in Hogwarts castle and other sets.

Wand
Wands are an essential accessory for any wizard! Adapted from LEGO Star Wars™ lightsabers, they also appear in black and grey.

Gold coins
These coins can be found throughout the LEGO Harry Potter sets, printed with values of 10, 20 and 30.

Spooky book

This LEGO book has unique printing on three sides. It belongs in the Restricted Section of Hogwarts library in set 4709.

Owl post

This envelope tile can be found in nine LEGO Harry Potter sets. Wizards and witches write a lot of letters!

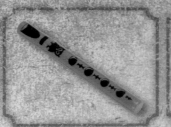

Flute

This LEGO wand piece has been decorated to become the flute that keeps Fluffy in a deep sleep in the Forbidden Corridor (set 4706).

Beater's bat

In Quidditch Match (set 4737) this element is a Beater's bat, but it can also be a carrot, or a torch with a flame!

The Quibbler

The Quibbler magazine tile appears in four sets, where the front page announces news about Harry Potter.

Hagrid's axe

Hagrid is the only Harry Potter minifigure to need an axe. This accessory is black in Hagrid's Hut (set 4754).

Remembrall

Neville Longbottom's Remembrall shows him when he's forgotten something. It is made from a transparent LEGO minifigure head piece, with swirling gold and silver patterns, and is found in Flying Lesson (set 4711).

Flying key

LEGO feathers were added to standard keys to make the winged keys for set 4704.

Magnifying glass

In Snape's Class (set 4705), this purple magnifying glass actually functions to magnify objects.

Hand of Glory

This light grey tile comes from Knockturn Alley (set 4720). The spooky printed hand is known as the Hand of Glory.

Trunk

This chest is a popular LEGO piece, and appears with Harry in The Knight Bus (set 4755) with luggage tiles inside.

Daily Prophet

The *Daily Prophet* tile features the latest wizarding news in the same four sets as *The Quibbler*.

Wormtail's dagger

Peter Pettigrew holds this sacrificial silver knife in set 4766.

Gregory Goyle
⇜ SLYTHERIN SIDEKICK ⇝

The updated version of Gregory Goyle, Draco Malfoy's crony, patrols the corridors of Hogwarts (set 4867). This minifigure's hair has a new style and colour. LEGO designers have revised the scowling expression from the 2002 variant (p.52).

Goyle now has a flat-top hair piece.

DATA FILE

SETS: 4867 Hogwarts (2011)
PIECES: 4
ACCESSORIES: Black wand

Goyle does not come with a double-sided head, so his face only has one gormless expression.

Goyle carries a black wand, ready to curse any unsuspecting Gryffindors.

Crumpled jumpers
LEGO designers have carried the details of all the Hogwarts uniforms onto the backs of the minifigure torsos. These details include the coloured house stripes and creases for the ill-fitting jumpers.

Goyle now wears black trousers instead of the grey ones worn by his earlier variant.

Professor Lupin
⸺ HOGWARTS DEFENDER ⸺

Lupin has a wavy dark orange hair piece.

The third variant of the werewolf Professor Lupin has the same hair piece as the original version (p.67), but his face and clothing have been updated. The former Defence Against the Dark Arts Professor is now ready to face the Death Eaters in the battle of Hogwarts.

Final Hogwarts
For the fifth version of Hogwarts (4867), LEGO designers recreated Professor Lupin's office and the Astronomy Tower, linked by the bridge.

The updated face is printed with even more scratch marks, plus a beard and a moustache.

DATA FILE
⸺◆◆◆⸺

SETS: 4867 Hogwarts (2011)
PIECES: 4
ACCESSORIES: Reddish-brown wand

Lupin is dressed in a dark tan suit with a tan shirt and dark brown tie.

Did you know?
A lever on Hogwarts (set 4867) causes the bridge to "explode", throwing minifigures into the air and revealing LEGO fire pieces underneath.

Narcissa Malfoy
MALFOY MATRIARCH

Narcissa Malfoy will do anything to protect her family. Dressed in an intimidating black outfit, her minifigure joins a group of Voldemort's followers that have captured Hagrid and are waiting for Harry Potter in The Forbidden Forest (set 4865).

Narcissa's head is double-sided. One side shows her unsmiling, while the other shows her baring her teeth in anger.

Narcissa's reddish-brown hair piece has two tan streaks in it. She is the only LEGO Harry Potter minifigure to have two-coloured hair.

Narcissa is armed with a black wand.

Dress detail
The rich embroidery of Malfoy's ornate dress is carried over onto the back of her torso. Her dress is very similar to the outfit worn by her sister, Bellatrix Lestrange (p.124).

DATA FILE

SETS: 4865 The Forbidden Forest (2011)
PIECES: 4
ACCESSORIES: Black wand

Lord Voldemort
⟶ HARRY'S NEMESIS ⟵

DATA FILE

SETS: 4842 Hogwarts Castle (2010), 4865 The Forbidden Forest (2011)
PIECES: 4
ACCESSORIES: Cloak, white wand

As part of the final battle at Hogwarts, LEGO designers updated the minifigure of Lord Voldemort, making him more malevolent and evil than ever. His mad, staring eyes are now fixed on one goal – defeating Harry Potter!

This version of Voldemort shows the Dark Lord baring his teeth in a hideous grin.

Forbidden Forest
The Dark Lord is found as part of set 4865 where he waits in the Forbidden Forest for Harry Potter to fight him. Close by is one of his Horcruxes, the slithering serpent Nagini.

Voldemort wears a standard black LEGO cloak that is found on 44 other minifigures across the LEGO universe.

Index

DK

LONDON, NEW YORK, MELBOURNE, MUNICH AND DELHI

Editorial Assistant Emma Grange
Designer Jon Hall
Managing Art Editor Ron Stobbart
Publishing Manager Catherine Saunders
Art Director Lisa Lanzarini
Publisher Simon Beecroft
Publishing Director Alex Allan
Production Editor Clare McLean
Production Controller Melanie Mikellides

For Tall Tree:
Editors David John, Rob Colson
Designers Ed Simkins, Jonathan Vipond, Ben Ruocco
Consultant Alastair Disley

Additional LEGO® Harry Potter™ minifigures photographed by Huw Millington

First published in Great Britain in 2012
by Dorling Kindersley Limited
80 Strand, London, WC2R 0RL

10 9 8 7 6 5 4 3 2 1
001—183845—Jun/12

Page design copyright © 2012 Dorling
Kindersley Limited

LEGO, the LEGO logo, the Brick and
Knob configurations, and the Minifigure
are trademarks of the LEGO Group.
©2012 The LEGO Group.
Produced by Dorling Kindersley Limited
under license from the LEGO Group.

A CIP catalogue record for this book is available
from the British Library.

ISBN: 978-1-40938-318-5

Colour reproduction by Media Development
Printing Ltd, UK
Printed and bound in China by Leo Paper
Products

Acknowledgements
Dorling Kindersley would like to thank Melanie Swartz, Victoria Selover,
Elaine Piechowski and Ashley Bol at Warner Bros.; Corinna Van Delden,
Randi Sørensen and Henrik Saaby Clausen at the LEGO Group; LEGO
Harry Potter collectors Huw Millington and Alastair Disley; Elizabeth
Dowsett for editorial support; The Blair Partnership and J. K. Rowling.

Discover more at
www.dk.com   www.LEGO.com   www.warnerbros.com